MW01166754

Audiophile's Guide

The Stereo

Unlock the Secrets to Great Sound

by Paul McGowan

Copyright © 2020 Paul McGowan.

All rights reserved. No part of this publication may be reproduced, distributed, or transmitted in any form or by any means, including photocopying, recording, or other electronic or mechanical methods, without the prior written permission of the publisher, except in the case of brief quotations embodied in critical reviews and certain other noncommercial uses permitted by copyright law. For permission requests, write to the publisher, addressing your request to "Attention: Permissions Coordinator," at the address below.

ISBN: 9798592447990

Front cover image by Laura Duffy
Illustrations by James Whitworth
Edited by Dr. John Acker

First printing edition 2020

Viceroy Press LLC
4865 Sterling Drive
Boulder, Colorado 80301

www.audiophilesguide.com

www.psaudio.com

The Author

Paul McGowan is the CEO and co-founder of PS Audio®, a world-renowned designer and manufacturer of high-end stereo equipment. He is also the bestselling author of the book 99% True and a popular YouTube presenter, with more than 130,000 subscribers.

With over 45 years of experience designing, engineering, and crafting hundreds of high-end audio products, ranging from phono preamplifiers to exotic digital audio innovations, Paul has helped build a strong community of audiophiles and stereo lovers around the world.

Paul and his wife Terri, along with their four sons and many grandchildren, live and work in beautiful Boulder, Colorado, where they enjoy a robust outdoor lifestyle of hiking, biking, skiing, and of course, listening to great music.

Join our family

At PS Audio, we're family. Not just a family that runs in bloodlines, but in frequencies. Because while we may not all share the same genes here, we are all related by a passion, nay, obsession with listening to the music we love at the highest, most breathtaking quality possible.

And in our minds, that makes us kin.

That's how we've built our company over the last 45 years - with the kind of care and respect that you give to your family.

Join us.

www.psaudio.com

Also by Paul McGowan ...

It's 99% True...

Paul McGowan tells all (and then some) in this riotous tale of misbegotten success that's 99% true in all the best ways. From his not-so-innocent youth growing up in the shadow of Disneyland and summer evenings in the innocent 1950s, to his dope-smoking, snake-eating, draft-dodging, loony-bin misadventure through Europe, to his struggles to build a thriving enterprise from a stack of dusty albums. Come enjoy funny bone laughs and heartrending stories as Paul tries to find his place in the worldwide community of High-End Audio.

Available on Amazon or www.psaudio.com for a hand-signed copy from the author.

Contents

Introduction

I've spent most of my adult life deeply involved with the reproduction of music in the home. I come by it honestly: from my earliest childhood memories, my father Don's handcrafted Hi-Fi system filled the McGowan household with the sounds of Louis Armstrong, Sarah Vaughn, Louis Prima, Keely Smith, and Sam Butera and The Witnesses. Dad cobbled together bits and pieces of monophonic Hi-Fi components to build the snazziest music system in our neighborhood, though his enthusiasm for Hi-Fi wasn't always shared by my mother Sue. I still remember how angry Mom got when Dad attacked the family's hall closet with saws, hammers, and drills to convert it to a subwoofer enclosure.

In my early college days, I too built my own Hi-Fi system, using Dad's pile of discarded equipment. But that was long ago when home music systems were monophonic: everything played through a single speaker. Just like black-and-white TV shows were considered completely normal before color televisions emerged, monophonic sound was the standard for home music reproduction. It was just the way you did it. It wasn't until the late 1960s and early 1970s that two-channel stereo crept into our lives, forever changing how we listen to music. Our world blossomed out of its black-and-white, monophonic innocence into breathtaking color and stereo realism.

Suddenly, home entertainment went from the quaint sidelines to being an increasingly urgent priority. Homes with color televisions jumped from 3 million in 1965 to well over 30 million just 6 years later. The smattering of monophonic home audio consoles like my dad's, carefully assembled in the 50s and 60s, hit the second-hand stores as a tsunami of stereo speakers and receivers washed over the US, Europe, and Asia. By the mid-1970s my generation of Baby Boomers had arrived with our bags of weed, our caches of albums, and our pairs of loudspeakers. Most of us, including me, didn't have much in the way of worldly possessions, but having a stereo was non-negotiable.

It was clear to me the first time I went from a single speaker Hi-Fi to two-channel stereophonic sound that two speakers outperformed one, simply filling the room better. But I had yet to grasp stereo sound's true potential. That revelatory moment came in 1973, on a hot summer's day in Santa Maria, California. I was working as a disc jockey and program director at a local FM radio station, and the station's chief engineer, Jim Mussell, invited me to his home to hear his stereo system. He knew I loved music and had heard me brag about my home audio setup. Given that my rig played loud rock, impressed my friends, and had two tall loudspeakers, I felt pretty confident that I was in the upper echelon of stereo aficionados. I was soon to learn otherwise.

Jim lived in a modest three-bedroom track home on the east side of Santa Maria, near the noisy 101 freeway. His home was a hoarder's dream, filled with stacks of papers, test equipment, and piles of boxes kissing the ceiling. From the front door we wound our way through the chaotic maze and into a surprisingly neat and orderly living room. Wedged into each of the room's two far corners was a 4x4' dark mahogany speaker cabinet. In their center was a two-foot-wide and three-foot-tall panel of dark wood, flanked on each side by black grille cloth. Near the very top of the center block was what looked to me like window louvers.

The author in 1973 at KXFM Radio, Santa Maria,

These two cabinets, explained Jim, were his pride and joy: an original pair of JBL D30085 Hartsfield corner horn loudspeakers. On the table to the left side of the room sat a fancy looking turntable, with an unusual arm that moved straight across the album instead of the typical pivoting tonearm. And next to that was an ancient looking Audio Research preamplifier with *vacuum tubes* (of all things). I remember quietly snickering at the use of these ancient fire bottle vacuum tubes—my dad had used them, for Pete's sake, but *I* had long since graduated to the newer transistor models. All Jim had was an ancient pair of loudspeakers coupled with old amp technology...and I was supposed to be impressed?! Harrumph. As I sat in the single overstuffed chair facing the speakers, Jim lowered the needle onto Edgar Winter's *Frankenstein*. I did my best to be polite, pretending I was going to be impressed.

Holy shit. Suddenly, the musicians were in the room! No sound came from those two ancient speakers—instead, standing before me were Edgar Winter, Ronnie Montrose, Dan Hartman, and Chuck Ruff. Winter's synthesizer was alive and in three dimensions, while Ruff's drumbeats smacked me in the stomach and dropped my jaw to my chest. It was as if neither the room nor the speakers even existed. I was *there*, on a holographic soundstage. I could "see" where each musician stood on that stage and I could picture Winter's fingers gliding over the ARP keyboard he slung across his chest and played like a guitar. Hartman's bass notes went lower than I ever imagined possible, at least outside of a live performance.

JBL Hartsfield Corner Horn loudspeaker

When the final synth note died away in the reverb chamber, I turned to look at my friend. Jim seemed unfazed by what we had just experienced—as if it were just an everyday occurrence—and launched into some engineering techno-babble we two nerds had previously been chatting about. I cannot remember a word he'd said, though, because I was still digesting the life-changing experience.

I had gone from flat monotone to three-dimensional color in the four minutes and forty-four seconds it took Edgar and his group to play that song. The idea that two speakers could disappear from the room—and that in their place live musicians might appear to play music—was so mind-bendingly new that I struggled to wrap my head around it. What made this magic? Was it those speakers? That odd turntable? The vacuum tubes? His room? All of it? I had to know. 46 years later, after a lifetime of designing equipment, building stereo systems, and helping audiophiles around the world achieve what I experienced on that hot summer's day, I feel pretty confident I can help you achieve that same sense of wonder and amazement that forever changed my life.

The Audiophile's Guide will be a series of books designed to help music lovers get all that is possible out of their stereo systems. This first book, *The Stereo*, will give you the basic tools you need to experience three-dimensional audio, the kind where the speakers disappear and the musicians are playing in the room. Future books will dive deeper into specific techniques, for those of you who want to continue the journey of faithfully reproducing live music in your home. So, if you want to experience that same life-changing event that I did nearly a half century ago, then hop in. Together, we're going to make music come alive.

A Brief History of Stereophonic Sound

On April 10, 1940, the *New York Times* ran the headline: "*Sound Waves 'Rock' Carnegie Hall...Tones Near Limit at what the Human Ear Can Endure.*"
The article went on,

> "*The loudest musical sounds ever created crashed and echoed through venerable Carnegie Hall last night as a specially invited audience listened, spellbound, and at times not a little terrified.*"

This spectacle was largely facilitated by Harvey Fletcher, a psychoacoustician and the Acoustical Society's first president. Fletcher stood at a control panel in Carnegie Hall, fine-tuning recordings of the Philadelphia Orchestra (playing under the direction of his long-time collaborator, Leopold Stokowski) that were being piped into the auditorium.

The two friends were demonstrating "enhanced" music, in which the dynamic range of the recordings had been drastically expanded during production for a dramatic effect that could literally bowl over an unprepared listener. At Stokowski's command, the sound level shifted across a range of nearly 100 dB; at its loudest, the wall of sound emanating from the three loudspeakers positioned on the stage was comparable to the output of 2,000 musicians. "When he wanted a stupefying volume of tone, that in Carnegie Hall seemed to shake the building, he got it instantly," reported the *Times*.

Leopold Stokowski with Dr. Harvey Fletcher

But the demonstration was not merely a show of power. Although the music was played through three enormous loudspeakers, sheathed in a curtain of fabric to hide the sound's origins, the performance sounded as if it were really happening on stage, with the bass coming from one side and the violins from another. This remarkable auditory illusion of stereophonic sound was the careful work of Fletcher and his team of engineers from Bell Telephone Laboratories, who in turn relied on all the audio pioneers who came before them.

The road that leads us from Edison's tin-foil cylinder to today's high-end two-channel stereo systems—and beyond—is a fascinating avenue crammed with remarkable people, inventions, and innovations. Our past accomplishments contribute to what we are today, and signpost the future as a never-ending quest to push the envelope of what is possible in audio.

What is Stereophonic Sound?

Stereophonic sound creates an illusion of location for various instruments within the original recording, in the same way that stereoscopic images give us the illusion of three-dimensional space. A well-configured high-end stereo system can offer an uncanny three-dimensional audio experience in your home. On a proper system, listeners can achieve an audio experience that is convincing enough to make them believe the vocalist or musicians are actually in the room, allowing them to form an emotional and visceral connection to the music and what the artist intended. Most people have never heard a good audiophile stereo system, let alone one that produces a three-dimensional image: the two speakers disappear acoustically, and instead the notes coming from the drummer, guitarist, vocalist, or other musicians appear between, beside, and behind where the speakers are set up, creating a seamless soundstage.

Once listeners get to hear what a well-placed speaker pair powered by proper electronics can produce, there's no going back. The opportunity to bring the illusion of live musicians into the home at the touch of a button, the twist of a knob, or the swipe of a finger—from online libraries so massive you couldn't exhaust them in a lifetime of listening—is addictive.

IN THE BEGINNING

French inventor, Clément Ader is credited with demonstrating the first two-channel audio system, in 1881. He used a series of telephone transmitters connected from the stage of the Paris Opera to a suite of rooms at the Paris Electrical Exhibition, where listeners could hear a live transmission of performances through receivers for each ear. *Scientific American* reported:

Clement Ader

> *Every one who has been fortunate enough to hear the telephones at the Palais de l'Industrie has remarked that, in listening with both ears at the two telephones, the sound takes a special character of relief and localization which a single receiver cannot produce. [...] This phenomenon is very curious, it approximates to the theory of binauricular audition, and has never been applied, we believe, before to produce this remarkable illusion to which may almost be given the name of auditive perspective.*

This two-channel telephonic process was commercialized in France from 1890 to 1932 as the Théâtrophone, and in England from 1895 to 1925 as the Electrophone. Both were services available by coin-operated receivers at hotels and cafés, or by subscription to private homes.

MODERN STEREOPHONIC SOUND

Modern stereophonic technology was invented in the 1930s by British engineer Alan Blumlein at EMI, who patented stereo records, stereo films, and also surround sound. Blumlein was born on June 29, 1903, in London.

His future career seemed to have been determined by the age of seven, when he presented his father Semmy with an invoice for repairing the doorbell, signed "Alan Blumlein, Electrical Engineer" (with "paid" scrawled in pencil). His sister claimed that he could not read proficiently until he was 12. He replied "no, but I knew a lot of quadratic equations!"

Alan Blumlein

Blumlein was a lover of music. He tried to learn to play the piano, but he gave it up and switched to engineering. At the age of 28, his work at the Columbia Graphophone Company (later EMI) gave him an opportunity to enhance audio production and make his mark in history, when he invented what he called "binaural sound"—now known as stereophonic sound. The story goes something like this. In early 1931, Blumlein and his wife Doreen were at the cinema. The sound reproduction systems of the early talkies only had a single set of speakers—the actor might be on one side of the screen, but the voice could come from the other. Blumlein declared to his wife that he had found a way to make the sound follow the actor. He later patented his ideas with the title "Improvements in and relating to Sound-transmission, Sound-recording and Sound-reproducing Systems," The application was dated December 14, 1931, and it was accepted six months later as UK patent number 394,325.

Blumlein was killed in the crash of an H2S-equipped *Handley Page Halifax* test aircraft, while making a test flight for the Telecommunications Research Establishment (TRE) on June 7, 1942. During the flight from RAF Defford, while at an altitude of 500 ft, the *Halifax* developed an engine fire which rapidly grew out of control. The aircraft was seen to lose altitude, then rolled inverted and struck the ground, killing all those aboard.

STEPPING INTO BIG SHOES

Meanwhile, in the United States, physicist Harvey Fletcher of Bell Laboratories—the "father of stereophonic sound" who would later go on to rock Carnegie Hall—was beginning his push to extend the boundaries established by Blumlein even further.

On the evening of April 27, 1933, seven years prior to his Carnegie Hall event, Fletcher, ever the showman, welcomed a distinguished crowd to Constitution Hall in Washington, DC. Under the auspices of the National Academy of Sciences, an audience of presidential advisors, senators, and congressional representatives had gathered for a musical performance they assumed to be live. In the first act of the show, played through hidden speakers behind a curtain on the Washington, DC stage, the audience listened to a scene wired from Pennsylvania to Washington. On the left-hand side of the stage in Philadelphia, a handyman constructed a box with a hammer and saw. From the far right, another worker proffered suggestions to his friend. "So realistic was the effect," wrote an observer, "that to the audience in Washington the

Stokowski at the controls while Harvey Fletcher watches

act seemed to be taking place on the stage before them. Not only were the sounds of sawing, hammering, and talking faithfully reproduced through the hidden speakers, but the auditory perspective enabled the listeners to place each sound in its proper positions, and to follow the movements of the actors by their footsteps and voices." Next, a soprano sang "Coming Through the Rye" as she weaved her way across the stage in Philadelphia. At Constitution Hall, the phantom of her voice "appeared to be strolling on the stage."

The show ended with an unforgettable duel in the dark between two trumpet players separated by more than a hundred miles. The two traded licks from their opposite posts in Constitution Hall and the Academy of Music in Philadelphia. But the audience was none the wiser: "To those in the audience there seemed to be a trumpet player at each side of the stage before them. It was not until after the stage was lighted that they realized only one of the trumpet players was there in person." The crowd was in awe.

This was not simply a show of tricks. It was the grand public unveiling of Fletcher's ambitious and laborious project, stereophonic sound, which he had first learned from Blumlein. Thanks to the work of Fletcher, the world was now hearing more than their home monophonic sound systems could ever deliver. Stereophonic sound had begun to reach the masses—and they couldn't get enough.

Stereo Tsunami

By the 60s and 70s, legions of stereo systems hit the mass market, popularized by waves of Japanese receivers: single-unit stereo systems that combined a stereo preamplifier, power amplifier, and radio tuner in one box. These receivers, coupled with a flood of low-cost loudspeakers, soon became staples in homes across the world. The stereo revolution had taken over and the vinyl LP, stereo tape cassette, and stereo FM radio broadcasts, reigned on high.

Hi-Fi stereo dealers and manufacturers, drunk on their success selling sound systems to millions around the world, even tried to expand the number of speakers from two to four via a short-lived technology known as Quad-raphonic Sound. Quadraphonic audio was the earliest consumer product offering surround sound, which would one day become popular in home and commercial movie theaters, but in the 70s it was a commercial failure due to its many technical problems and format incompatibilities. Quadraphonic audio formats were more expensive to produce than standard two-channel stereo. Playback required additional speakers, along with specially designed decoders and amplifiers, at a time when people were still getting used to the idea of tolerating two speakers and a receiver in their living rooms. But stereo and its ability to produce a three-dimensional image in the home was here to stay, and it was the odd home that didn't sport a pair of speakers and a row of vinyl stereo LPs.

How it All Changed

The world's first commercial CD player, the Sony CDP-101

With the introduction of the Stereo Compact Disc (CD) on August 17, 1982, home stereo reproduction made another fundamental shift, this time in both form and technology. No longer were we scraping needles across a 12" plastic disc. The CD was something new—a 4.7" optical disc that needed a laser to do its work. We had entered the era of digital audio.

The first commercially available stereo CD player, the iconic Sony CDP-101, was offered by the electronics giant in Japan in October 1982. Born, as Sony states, nearly 100 years after the first phonograph player, the CDP-101 made its way to the US (and across the globe) around six to seven months after its initial debut in 1983, where it was priced as high as $1,000.

Following an initial offering of around 20 available discs at launch, the CD format exploded over the next few years. As reported by *The Guardian*, its unofficial arrival came with the release of Dire Straits' *Brothers in Arms* album, which was recorded on the latest digital equipment and spawned a tour sponsored by Philips. Released on CD in May 1985, the hit album became a musical mainstay, and vinyl fans and audiophiles began to purchase CD players in droves to adopt the growing format. By 1988, CD sales had eclipsed vinyl and they overtook the cassette in 1991.

In 1999, just as Millennials and the internet itself were coming of age, Napster hit the web and changed the world forever. Again. Allowing a network of global users to easily share music files, the site boomed, forcing the Recording Industry Association of America (RIAA) and other major industry organizations to

Original Gen 1 Apple iPod

scramble to catch up (and fetch their high-dollar lawyers). At its height Napster hosted around 80 million users, and it paved the way for other peer-to-peer sites like LimeWire, uTorrent, and many more. While Napster was eventually shuttered in 2001, the genie was out of the bottle, so to speak, and the piles of cash that CD sales had hauled in began to slowly but surely fade away.

In October 2001, amid this confluence of assaults on the beleaguered CD, Apple's forward-sighted innovator Steve Jobs unleashed perhaps his greatest creation to that point: the gorgeous little MP3 player known as the iPod. In true Apple fashion, the iPod was far from the first of its kind—and some might argue it wasn't even the best—but paired with Apple's new iTunes music app, the iPod took the world by storm and became the must-have music accessory. Perhaps just as striking, iTunes sales became a musical powerhouse for Apple, engorging its coffers and changing the way people purchased music—for those who still did pay for it. In 2005, iTunes outpaced CD sales in two major physical stores for the first time. But that modest victory would be short-lived.

Pandora's inception in January 2000 spawned from the Music Genome Project, an "internet radio" service following an algorithm that categorizes music with hundreds of characteristics, allowing it to serve listeners music they'll like based upon artists, songs, and simple thumbs-up or thumbs-down ratings. The first major on-demand service, Spotify, came eight years later, and together, the two companies helped rewrite the music playbook. Offering free/affordable music to anyone online—without the need to break the law or store massive amounts of data—music streaming quickly became an industry giant. In 2014, streaming revenue eclipsed CD sales for the first time, and it did the same for digital downloads in 2015.

HERE'S WHERE WE COME IN

From Edison's famous "Mary had a little lamb" speech, recorded on a tin-foil-layered spinning disc, to making the world's music available in stereo at the touch of a finger, stereophonic sound is here to stay. For those lucky enough to have enjoyed the wonders of a properly set up audiophile two-channel system, there are few joys greater than the enjoyment of music in the home. Ready to roll up your sleeves and pull off one of the great magic tricks of all time—making your speakers disappear and, with the lights on low, create the three-dimensional illusion of musicians sharing the room with you?

Ready?

Before We Get Started...

The Audiophile's Guide *The Stereo* depends on having access to a copy of *Reference Music* from Octave Records. This reference disc, available as an SACD (compatible with all CD and DVD players), a download, as well as a limited edition vinyl record, is an invaluable tool referenced multiple times during both the Basic as well as Advanced setup chapters.

While certainly you can use other reference materials, you'll get the best results if you follow our step-by-step instructions using this reference disc.

Reference Music is available from Octave Records at www.psaudio.com. You may order online or call 800PSAUDIO

The Audiophile

OPEN EARS

WEEKEND SMILE

AUDIOPHILE GUIDE

DEFINITIVE AUDIO SET-UP BOOK

TAPE MEASURE

M ost people only need a simple sound system to bring the joy of music into their homes—even Sonos, Amazon Echo, or Apple HomePod can fill the room with tunes. But for audiophiles like me, and hundreds of thousands more across the globe, the lifeless two-dimensional facsimiles that these middle-of-the-road consumer offerings present soon start to grate on our nerves. At best they do a disservice to the music's tonal truth, only scratching the surface of the musical experience possible with the right technical setup.

On today's smart speaker audio systems, a big orchestral piece by the likes of Gustav Mahler or Ludwig van Beethoven does not sound live. They are so far away from suspending disbelief as to be laughable. Our brains immediately reject the suggestion that an orchestra is in the room, as these puny speakers or MP3 players struggle to present the combined sound of 100 musicians performing together in a massive music hall.

The questionable performance of low-end consumer audio products is not news to the experienced audiophile, but perhaps this is your first toe dip into the world of high-end audio. If so, I welcome you.

In our world, the challenge of a good two-channel audio system is to recreate the sound of live musicians in the room with you—to convince you to suspend disbelief, if only for a few minutes. Turn the lights down low and the objects making the music—the speakers—disappear, leaving only a 3D recreation of the players, as if they were on an imaginary soundstage behind those speakers. First-time listeners to a well-designed, high-end stereo system are often stunned at the gap between what they hear and what they expect from a consumer-level system. What advanced audiophiles understand is that a great stereo doesn't have to cost an arm and a leg. With proper equipment selection and setup, amazingly lifelike music can be a part of anyone's home.

By following this guide you can bring magic to your HiFi system

Hearing the Difference

Right now, beginning audiophile readers of the *Guide* might be wondering something important: "if I invest in a high-end stereo, will I really be able to hear the difference?" I get that question a lot. On more occasions than I can count, I've brought the uninitiated or seemingly uninterested into our music rooms at PS Audio. Everyone—from the UPS driver to the fire extinguisher inspector—left the room with their jaw hanging open. None had ever known a stereo system could produce sound so lifelike, even the ones used to a good stereo system. Those few minutes of listening opened their eyes—or ears in this case—to a whole new quality of sound. "It's as if the musicians are in the room" is the most common comment we get from first-time listeners to the PS Audio Reference System.

Whether you are a beginning or an advanced audiophile, once you follow the setup guide in these pages, you too will be able to get closer to the sound of live music on the right recordings (and perhaps even drop a few jaws yourself). Even if you're blessed with golden ears, the difference between live and recorded music starts to vanish when you are listening on a system that has been set up properly.

BUILDING A HIGH-END SYSTEM

The audiophile's world is all about achieving musical pleasure through an extraordinary home reproduction system—we're talking about music lighting up our lives. Achieving audiophile-grade performance requires a level of commitment greater than just walking into a Hi-Fi shop or thumbing through an equipment catalog. How much you get out of your music system often depends on what

Bring the sound of the musicians into your room as if they were live

you're willing to invest in both time and money. It helps to ask yourself a few questions to see just how deep you're prepared to dive.

How much are you willing to commit to the end goal of bringing high-performance audio into your home? If it's of casual interest to you, that's just fine—I pass no judgment whatsoever, and assure you that we can take what you have and improve it using just a few hours of your time. If, on the other hand, you're a beginning audiophile lusting after your own dose of that magic, or an advanced audiophile looking to squeeze more out of your curated system, then let's get down to business. Wringing out the best possible sound from your equipment will require effort and a level of commitment greater than just setting down speakers, connecting wires, and pressing *play*.

Your level of commitment will help determine how far you get in your quest for better sound

Whether you are at one of these two extremes or somewhere in the middle, I can help you reach your goals, and I have organized the next several chapters so that you can quickly find the information that's right for you. We will start with the basics of budget, move on to the room, equipment choices, and speaker setup, then follow that with a focus on tuning, to help you get a level of performance from your rig you may not have known was possible. You can stop there, grab a glass of vino and a plate of cheese and crackers, turn the lights down low, press play or lower the needle gently into the groove, and enjoy sound you didn't know your system could produce.

Should you wish to take it to a higher level, the advanced chapters will walk you through the finer details of tuning the room, selecting music that matters, arranging your

cables, tweaking your power sources, and everything else
that goes into building a fine system worthy of your time.
Whatever level you wish to work at, *The Audiophile Guide*
is here to help you through it.

"Music is a way to dream together and go to another dimension."

Cecilia Bartoli

The Budget

The cost of building a high-performance, audiophile-grade two-channel stereo system can span quite a range, from next to nothing to more than the cost of some homes. I'll let you in on a secret, though: there's often little correlation between stereo cost and performance.

In the half-century I've devoted to the high-end audio industry, I have heard every manner of system. Some of the very worst have been the most expensive and some of the best were quite affordable. Like anything else in our lives, simply throwing money at a problem or a project doesn't guarantee success. In fact, unless you are equipped with some basic knowledge, your investment may backfire. Without adequate information, preferably coupled with a knowledgeable, trusted guide to steer you in the right direction, plowing your hard-earned money into a two-channel audio system can be a real crapshoot.

When someone asks me what equipment to buy, I start with a series of three questions: 1) What are your goals? 2) What are your limitations? 3) What is your budget? Let's follow that same process here.

WHAT ARE YOUR GOALS AND LIMITATIONS?

This simple question is often the hardest for people to answer, or at least to put into words. Typical answers range from a simple "just give me good sound" to "I want the biggest, baddest, most bone-rattlingly killer sound system on the planet." These answers are adequate to get us started, but the real answers I am looking for would go something closer to this:

Like anything in our lives, simply throwing money at a problem doesn't guarantee success

"AFTER A SEARCH DOWN THE BACK OF THE COUCH I CAN OFFER YOU THREE BOTTLE TOPS, TWO PENNIES AND THE OSMONDS ON 8-TRACK."

"I am hoping to set up a modest system in my living room that the family can easily use for everyday listening, and on occasion, I want to crank it up and have it sound like there's a rock band playing in my living room."

Or:

"I'm looking for a small, unobtrusive set of speakers to go on either side of my television—something that can render classical and jazz in lifelike proportions and that I can easily switch to play the television audio."

Or:

"I want a no-holds-barred high-end system that just blows me and my friends away."

The trick to getting what you want is to first have a reasonably clear idea what that is

Answers like these give me a better idea of where to point you in terms of equipment choices and budget.

To help you understand how this can be applied in the real world, let me tell you about my own home setup. While at work, I get to enjoy one of the greatest high-performance two-channel reference systems in the world, PS Audio's Music Room Two, but at home it's a different story. My wife, Terri, wanted to build our home system herself. Since she too loves music and high-performance audio, I took her through my three questions to help identify her priorities. Her answers looked something like this:

Our home system is affordable yet high-performance

Goals:
- Turntable-based system with the ability to stream radio, Pandora, Tidal, and Qobuz
- Full range but it'll never be played at live concert levels
- Speakers need to sonically disappear
- Limitations:
- Must be small in footprint and not intrusive on the décor
- Must be simple to operate so even our grandkids can use it
- Budget:
- $4,000 maximum

With these answers in mind, it was easy for Terri to start her search and come up with her dream system. Here's what she ended up with:
- Turntable: Rega P3 with MM cartridge $1,100
- Amplifier: PS Audio Sprout $699

- Speakers: KEF LS50 $1,200
- Subwoofer: REL T5i $600
- Cables: $200
- System total: $3,800 or so

This system images beautifully, sounds great, and achieves Terri's goals. Had she been a little less particular about primarily playing vinyl records, she could have gotten the same quality at an even lower cost. For example, for those looking for a primarily streaming music system, at PS Audio we often pair our Sprout Integrated Amplifier with Elac speakers from Germany for under $1,000.

So, step one is to think about what you hope to achieve with your system. In other words, write down your goals. Step two factors in your limitations, such as where the system will be placed and how much real estate and visual prominence you and your significant other are willing to cede to the system. Once you've identified the answers to these two important questions, we can move on to the third question of budget. How much are you willing to invest in great sound?

WHAT IS YOUR BUDGET?
Now that you've identified your goals and limitations, let's talk budget. I've broken down system types into three general categories: the Casual System, the Serious System, and the Whacked-Out System. For a point of reference, my home system that I just described might fall into the upper end of the Casual System category, while the PS Audio Reference System would most certainly land in the Whacked-Out category.

Though it may seem counter intuitive, knowing what not to buy is often more helpful

WHAT NOT TO BUY

Before we get into system specifics, it's important to distinguish what I mean by a high-end two-channel stereo system from what the general population might consider to be "high-end." These days, you can find impressive-looking stereo equipment at big-box stores like Best Buy, large furniture outlets, and even Walmart or Target. Their systems mostly consist of a receiver—a fancy all-in-one box with everything you need except the speakers—from a big-name manufacturer like Sony, Yamaha, Marantz, Denon, and so on. Salespeople will assure potential buyers that this is the crème de la crème, as high-end as it gets. It can do 12-channel surround sound, has a radio tuner, pumps out lots of watts, features plenty of bells and whistles, and, according to them, is pretty much God's gift to music. If someone is trying to sell you one of these Swiss Army Knives of stereos, I suggest you run away as fast as you can. *A piece of equipment that does everything generally does nothing well.* Big box retailers' stereos

Don't be fooled by the glitz, bells and whistles of receivers with all their features

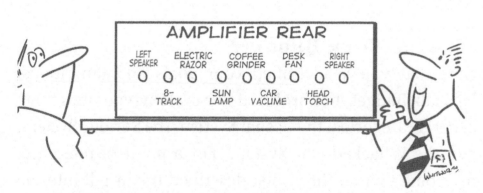

"THIS ONE IS GREAT - LOOK AT
ALL THE CONNECTIONS."

might be fine for home theaters and casual listening, but when it comes to rendering musical truth, they generally aren't in the same league.

Here's a tip: take a look at the unit's rear panel. If it bristles with more connectors and gadgets than you have any idea what to do with, leave it for someone else. You're not going to fall into that trap.

CASUAL SYSTEMS

The vast majority of serious two-channel audio systems would fall into this first category. We want great sound and we're willing to spend a few bucks and invest a few hours of setup to get there.

WHAT TO BUY

For a Casual System, you should plan to budget between $1,000 and $5,000 for everything you need. Next, select the various pieces of equipment from trusted manufacturers of two-channel separates. You'll be able to identify these manufacturers because:

- They don't make the receivers you're running away from
- You've done a little homework, by reading this book, to find out whether or not they are invested in bringing life to music
- Their products are purpose-built, to provide a specific outcome for a limited set of variables
- They are respected by the greater high-end audio community
- Their stated goals are to honor musical truth

Regardless of what level of system you choose to work towards, they all can bring magic

SERIOUS SYSTEMS

Serious Systems are more committed to a single person listening with intent. Their primary purpose is to help the listener forge a more intimate connection with the music than is possible with the Casual system, recreating a more believable live performance in the home. That means they require more money to build, more space in the room to place, and more time and care to set up.

WHAT TO BUY

For the Serious System you'll need to budget between $3,000 and $30,000 for everything you need. Now, for those unfamiliar with high-end audio, 30,000 smackaroos might at first seem like either a misprint or insanity, but I assure you, among audiophiles it's a perfectly normal investment. The average Serious System falls somewhere in the middle of this price range, hovering between $8,000 and $15,000, though I've heard some great Serious Systems that people cobbled together for around $8,000.

Next, select the various pieces of equipment from trusted manufacturers of two-channel separates. You'll be able to identify these manufacturers because:

- They don't make the receivers you're running away from
- Their products are purpose-built, to provide a specific outcome for a limited set of variables
- They are respected by the greater high-end audio community
- Their stated goals are to honor musical truth

Achieving great sound doesn't require a great deal of money. What's important is HOW you spend it

WHACKED-OUT SYSTEMS

As the name of this genre implies, the sky's the limit. I've seen some seriously unbelievable setups exceeding a million dollars, but, for the most part, you could put together a beautiful and impressive rig for as low as $15,000. More likely, though, the sweet spot's going to start at $25,000 or so.

The key for a Whacked-Out System to be worth its cost in both time and effort requires skill, knowledge, and tireless effort in addition to going for the cost-is-no-object components that synergistically mesh into audio nirvana. This level of system needs a personal guide and is certainly not for the faint at heart. Once built and experienced, there's few pleasures on Earth that compare.

WHAT TO BUY

For the Whacked-Out System you'll need to budget at least $25,000 and more likely closer to $50,000 and up. It's rare that all the components in these upper-end systems are sourced from one manufacturer. Perhaps the electronics are of the same breed, but then the loudspeakers, cables, AC power components, room and tuning products are likely from a variety of vendors. In these systems, everything matters. Components are chosen for performance as well as synergy within the chain.

Few manufacturers produce components worthy of a whacked-out system, though claims to the contrary often overwhelm one's search for the perfect component. Aside from a great deal of research via forums, reviews, audio tradeshows, and connections to others with similar goals, a personal guide is really helpful (that's my goal through

Making an intimate connection with the soul of the music is one of the more rewarding benefits of a stereo system

this series of books). These guides can also be found at the companies making the components, a trusted dealer, or a fellow traveler along the path to audio nirvana.

THE BOTTOM LINE

Truly great sound can be obtained in your home for under $1,000. It's not all about the money! It's far more important to understand what you want to achieve, then approach it methodically to make the most efficient use of your money, your time, and the real estate in your home you're willing to devote to music.

If you let me help you, I'll make sure you get the right equipment to meet your goals at a price you're comfortable paying, and then we're going to have fun setting it up and maximizing the music's potential.

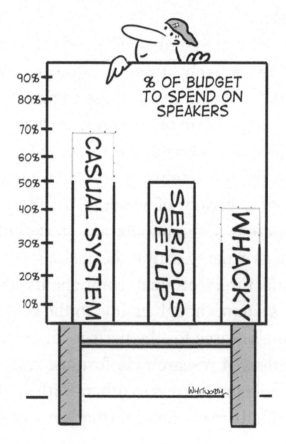

The Room

When building a two-channel audio system you have a number of choices for its location, from a casual bedroom system to a full-scale, money-is-no-object dedicated listening room. For many readers of this book, the choice of rooms has already been made—they have an existing system and purchased The Audiophile's Guide to improve it. If that's you, feel free to skip ahead to the next chapter.

For everyone else, the task ahead is to figure out where you want to build your system. In this chapter, I'll describe what these various choices look like and offer a quick overview of what's involved with each. From there, your task will be to choose which room you'd like to set up your system in. Once you've decided, I'll help you realize your dream.

Most of the world's high-end audio systems are located in the living room

THE LIVING ROOM SYSTEM

The living room is a classic venue for a stereo installation. In my late 20s and early 30s, at the beginning of the 1970s, most of my friends had a turntable, a stack of vinyl records, loudspeakers, and the electronics to drive them. Not many of us had televisions—or money—but none were without that stereo system. Over time, TV edged out my classic 70s music setup, much like my youth gave way to silver hair and a midriff bulge. But music is still prominent in my living room, and perhaps in yours as well.

The living room, as its name implies, often bustles with life: it's where we hang out, watch Netflix, put up the Christmas tree, play Scrabble, and entertain our friends and family. It's also often a shared space, which is where two-channel stereo hopefuls run into a few roadblocks:

only so much precious real estate can be devoted to speaker boxes, wires, and electronics, especially if your housemates don't want the stereo to be the center of attention. To make life even more interesting, the decent-sized living room in American single-family homes is by no means a global norm. Living space is at a premium in most cultures, not to mention in most apartments.

There are some truly great living room systems in all cultures and room sizes, coexisting in harmony with the family's needs, but they tend to require compromise because living rooms are more multi-purpose than other room options. That said, the living room is where most of us are going to plop down our two-channel stereo system.

I am going to assume throughout the rest of this book that you've chosen the living room for your setup, but before you make that decision, let me share with you a few alternative choices.

THE CASUAL ROOM SYSTEM

In larger homes there's often a second shared living space called by a variety of names: Casual Room, Family Room, Rumpus Room, and so forth. For those fortunate enough to have a dedicated room for play, it's often easier to devote a greater percentage of this smaller room's real estate to a two-channel stereo system than in the larger multi-purpose living room. Generally these rooms serve as family retreats, safe from the slings and arrows of guests, friends, grandmas, grandpas, and Aunt Mabels.

Casual Room systems are almost always smaller than what might work in the living room, but size is not

Getting agreement on how much real estate is available for system can be a challenge

"LOOK ON THE BRIGHT SIDE – WE
ONLY NEED ONE SPEAKER TO
COVER THE LOUNGE AND
THE BEDROOM."

all-important when it comes to achieving high-end sound in the home. Over the past 46 years of being an audiophile, some of the finest systems I have heard were small, compact setups in medium-sized rooms, carefully curated for great performance.

One of the Casual Room's benefits, isolation, can also be a problem. Because Casual rooms are typically detached from the home's common areas, it's problematic to use that new two-channel wonder system for background music parties and social gatherings in the living room. This is an easy problem to solve with a bit of planning. Simply add to the living room an easy to operate background music system like a Sonos, Apple HomePod, or even a small bedroom-style two-channel

It's easy enough to throw in a quality everyday music system for the family

setup. These mini systems can work wonders for your guests (including Aunt Mabel), while removing the pressure for you to compromise the Casual room system.

Should you decide to go with the Casual room system approach, you're likely going to have fewer diplomatic hurdles to clear than those often encountered with living room systems.

BEDROOM, OFFICE, AND SMALL ROOM SYSTEMS

As rooms get smaller, it gets more challenging to craft high-performance two-channel stereo systems. But that doesn't mean they can't produce some wonderful music. You just need to be careful with your expectations, rely heavily upon building the proper synergy of equipment, and pay particular attention to the room itself.

While it is possible to get really good sound in a small bedroom or office, it's unrealistic to expect the overwhelming majesty of the larger listening rooms I described earlier. There are exceptions, of course, but to recreate a full orchestra or rock band within the confines of a small bedroom, you would likely have to convert the entire room into a small temple of sound. If you just add a two-channel audio system to an already cluttered bedroom, don't plan for the speakers to disappear and the orchestra to magically seem to float in that cramped space. But if you are leaning in the direction of a small-room setup, you should consider a near field system, which I'll likely expand upon in future volumes of the Guide.

The trick to building any system is understanding what is possible and being clear and realistic with your expectations of what you hope to achieve. Like much of

The smaller the room, the more difficult it becomes to capture the full essence of a live performance

engineering (and much of life, for that matter), building a two-channel stereo requires a series of compromises. I am here to help you unravel your choices, so you can make the right decisions to get what you hope to achieve. It's all possible, but some options are more difficult than others.

THE DEDICATED ROOM

Dedicated rooms can be in the attic, basement, over the garage, or anywhere big enough

Ah yes, finally we get to the dedicated high-end room, sometimes known (slightly tongue-in-cheek) as the Man Cave. A dedicated room can be just about anywhere in the home, but often it is found in the basement, over the garage, or in some cases as a purpose-built room for the perfection of two-channel audio. It's a temple of sound where every inch of the room is dedicated to the task at hand: bringing the sound of live music into the room like few on Earth have ever had the glorious opportunity to hear—in many respects exceeding that of a live performance.

Dedicated rooms can range from simple single-use spaces, with a living-room style two-channel stereo system, to magnificent palaces reflecting six-figure investments and years of fine-tuning. About 25 years ago, I traveled all the way to the Philippines to hear one such system, which was based on my company's (at the time) loudspeakers. These were the Genesis Is, 4 columns of speakers weighing 1.2 tons and purchased only by the most serious—or perhaps whacked-out—audiophiles on the planet. They are a more modern version of what we, at PS Audio, use for one of our own reference systems today: the mighty Infinity IRSV, an earlier 1.2-ton version of the 4-piece Genesis beauties. Here's what I experienced in my client's high-end listening room, excerpted from 99% True.

The Music Room couldn't have been smaller than 1,000 square feet — a single rectangular room with arched 20-foot ceilings and near-perfect acoustics. Its proportions felt comfortable. The minimal room treatments consisted of a series of diffuser panels — wall-mounted boxes filled with varying depths of vertical wooden slats stacked in a horizontal row, made of a tasteful dark wood and placed sparingly along the wall behind the listener, blending nicely into the wall's dark beige. The furniture was elegant, not overblown, as in some listening rooms I've seen, which seem to have been designed to impress the first-time visitor. This room had three chairs exactly one-third of the way into the room from the wall behind them. The backs of the chairs were no higher than a seated adult's shoulder blades, so as not to bounce sound back toward the listener's ears, and the central chair was in the sweet spot. In front of the center seat was a low coffee table, where rested a single remote control. A third of the way out into the room from the far wall, on thick, white, wall-to-wall carpet, stood a gorgeous pair of our big Genesis Is, their dark rosewood veneer gleaming from a recent cleaning. Between the speakers and listening seats spread a handwoven area rug of deep, elegant red. It was a perfect audio room, tastefully set up and appointed.

My host put on a CD: Cantate Domino,

This fellow's temple of sound was unlike anything I had ever seen or heard

Torsten Nilsson conducting Oscar's Motet Choir in an album of Christmas music. My favorite track, "Cantique de Noël," a version of "O Holy Night" sung in Swedish, is a soaring choral performance with pipe organ, recorded in 1976 by Bertil Alving in Oscar's Church, in Stockholm. This is a tough recording to reproduce properly because of the many voices and the large space the system is trying to recreate, and my host's confident smile told me that he knew it well.

I was gobsmacked by what I heard. Indeed, the room was perfect, the electronics were just right, and the interconnects and cables couldn't have been better. With the lights nearly out, I closed my eyes and seemed to be transported to Oscar's Church—a massive, three-aisle Gothic cathedral that can hold 1,200 people, has a tower 260 feet tall, and features one of the largest pipe organs in Europe, boasting 5,200 pipes. There was a ruffle of air on my back—the physically palpable sound of the deepest, largest notes of that massive pipe organ. Gruff and rumbling, it nearly lifted me off my seat. Then, as if heaven-directed, my soul was soothed by the delicate, honeyed voice of a soprano. My eyes were shut, but by sound alone I could picture the 260-foot-tall ceiling of stone arches and the 33 stained-glass windows of the Oscarskyrkan...

Everything about this room had been perfected

By now, you can see the range of possibilities for implementing a two-channel stereo system in your home. It's all about expectations and practical realities. Maybe you'll opt for a small bedroom system, an honored spot in the family's living or family room, or even an amazing one-of-a-kind dedicated listening room.

"Music is the divine way to tell beautiful, poetic things to the heart."

Pablo Casals

The Room: Friend, Foe, and Partner

One of the greatest puzzles in home audio reproduction turns out to be the room—that enclosed box we call home. As you'll learn in this chapter, rooms offer both benefits and problems when setting up a home audio system. The more you know about rooms and their interactions with the speakers, the more comfortable you will be setting up and troubleshooting your system.

The room is both our biggest benefit and nightmare all at the same time

OUR ROOMS AS FRIENDS

Without the benefit of a room to enclose the speakers' sound field, your stereo system would sound surprisingly empty and lifeless. Bass note levels would be greatly diminished, and more importantly any chance of forming a holographic soundstage would be gone.

To better understand the importance of the room, here's a simple experiment. Take any loudspeaker and compare how its music sounds indoors and outdoors. It's as easy as grabbing a small MP3 rig, your kid's boombox (Hmm, do kids still have boomboxes? And why won't they get off my lawn?), your laptop computer and speakers, or even a small bedroom stereo system. Play a track of music inside the room first, then try the same thing outside. You might be surprised at how naked it sounds. Stripped of any room reflections, music played outside sounds sterile, in the same way your voice does. Inside, your words resonate and fill the room, while outside they are weaker without the reinforcements provided by interior walls.

Rooms have hard, reflective surfaces like walls, ceilings, and floors that reinforce sound waves, so they don't dissipate as they would outside. Rooms also have objects that absorb and redistribute sounds, such as furniture,

"MEET MY BEST FRIEND, DEN –
HE'S ALWAYS THERE FOR ME,
IS ALWAYS HAPPY TO LISTEN,
AND NEVER JUDGES ME
WHEN I PLAY FRAMPTON
COMES ALIVE."

drapes, bookcases, and rugs, which helps keep those reflections from being too direct in any one plane. Between the reflective surfaces and obstructive objects, each enclosed space forms a distinctive sound signature: compare the hollow echo of the garage, with its hard concrete flooring, to the more controlled environment of a bedroom with its carpeted floor, soft bed, and curtained windows.

OUR ROOMS AS ENEMIES

As important as our rooms are for good sound, they are also our biggest problems. When we play music in a room, those helpful reflective surfaces also unnaturally mangle, muddle, distort, amplify, and otherwise rob the pristine soundwaves of their purity. Unlike a concert hall where the walls, ceiling, and floor reflections surrounding the orchestra empty into a large open space for the audience to enjoy, our rooms are more like enclosed boxes. Sound

Bass frequencies bunch up in the room's corners and surfaces, generating standing waves

waves bounce back and forth between surfaces in an acoustic jumble—bass frequencies build up huge pressure zones known as standing waves, while midrange and higher frequencies clatter about in a dizzying jumble of reflections that confuse the ear and wreak havoc on the sound.

For sure, there's a love/hate relationship between your room and its music reproduction system. You can't get what you want without the room, but all the room's aural problems can overwhelm its benefits. Fortunately, you have plenty of options for working with the room instead of just tolerating its weaknesses.

Accepting the problems found in every room is the first step to overcoming its challenges

Working with What You Have

Wherever you choose to place your high-performance home audio system, it's going to sound very different there than in any other room. Even given a perfect setup, each room's sonic signature is unique. That's one reason why the same equipment never quite sounds the same in two different rooms.

You have two main options here: accept your room as it is and try to work with the space (and perhaps compromise performance), or work with the room and try and mitigate some of its problems, turning vice into benefit. If time permits, I prefer to work with a room and use whatever tools I possess to help get the best possible sound.

Unifying the Room and the System

The best way to think about the room and your system is to treat them as a single entity, a pair of elements, instead of as antagonists. If you think of them not as battling factions but rather unwitting partners, you'll have a much easier time bringing the magic of a high-end stereo system to life.

By analogy, think about a car and its motor. An automobile's motor is a feat of engineering magnificence. Its sole purpose is to produce as much power as efficiently as possible—a thing of beauty when placed on the test bench. Saddle that motor with a few thousand pounds of dead weight from the automobile's cabin, though, and it struggles and strains to do its work. To make a great automobile, engineers must work with coach and motor alike to fashion a single perfect unit. The same is true for an audio system and the room it is playing in.

Now that we have an idea of what we're up against, let's take a look at some of the more specific problems presented by the room/stereo interface.

GETTING CORNERED

Perhaps the worst place for sound in any room is the corners. The meeting of two walls forms a kind of horn that amplifies some frequencies and not others. For example, stand in the middle of your room and start speaking, noting the tonal quality of your voice. Continue to speak as you approach the corner of your room. Notice the change in the tonal balance the closer you get to the corner. Lower frequencies become exaggerated relative to higher ones. This sounds very unnatural—the exact opposite of what we're hoping to achieve.

Don't place speakers or subwoofers in corners

Because of this horn-like quality of corners, you don't want to place most modern loudspeakers in the corner, though some older speakers were specifically designed for corner placement. Perhaps the most famous one was a folded, corner-horn loudspeaker which became known as the Klipschorn (the very same speaker I first heard in Santa Maria, California that started me on my stereo journey). All through the 50s, dozens of US manufacturers licensed Klipsch patents, and hobbyist publications were filled with ads for "Klipsch patent horn" enclosures and kits. But today's modern speakers were not designed for corner placement, so unless you own one of those classics, stay out of the corners. Just remember: your stereo is your baby, and nobody puts baby in the corner.

You can always build your system first, then later improve the room

HIDDEN CORNERS

The most obvious room corners are the points where two walls meet, but they are not the only corners you should be concerned with. Because rooms are typically longer and wider than they are tall, the longest corner surfaces tend to be where floors, ceilings, and walls meet. This increase in length means that the corner horn effect I mentioned earlier sounds quite different. Where a traditional corner forms a four-sided horn between floor, ceiling, and walls, the long junction of wall to floor and ceiling is less of an acoustic horn and more of a reverberant slap echo chamber.

As you walk the room, clap your hands near the room's boundaries. What you are hoping for is a clean slap without any lingering reverberant echoes. If you're starting with an empty room, chances are good that as you approach the wall boundaries, you will hear a sharp (sometimes repeating) echo retort to your hand clap, coming from the junctions between the ceiling, floor, and walls. This is known as a slap echo, something you want to eliminate.

Often, adding a floor covering and furniture will mitigate the slap echo, but some rooms need more. The floor-to-wall junctions are easy to work with, since the addition of carpet and physical objects such as bookshelves, tables, lamps, etc. will break up these slap echoes. The wall-ceiling junctions are more problematic, though. Here, you can reduce the 90° sharp meeting of wall and ceiling by adding some crown molding. This simple, decorative, angled piece of trim reduces unwanted slap echo, and in many cases, eliminates it altogether.

HOW FURNITURE HELPS ROOM ACOUSTICS

The easiest of all room treatment methods is the use of furniture and physical objects in the room. The various objects we loosely refer to as furniture can be broken into two main categories: absorptive and reflective.

Absorptive furniture, like a couch or stuffed chair, derives its name from the way it interacts with sound. Instead of sound bouncing off its surface as we might expect from a hard, reflective piece such as a picture, TV, or wooden chair, soft surfaces absorb audio sound waves by converting them to heat.

Now, this doesn't mean that your couch or favorite chair will get hot when you play your stereo system. But let me give you a quick physics lesson. Sound is the ordered movement of air molecules in rapid waving patterns, while heat is the disordered, random, movement of atoms and molecules. So, if you want to absorb sound you need to disrupt that orderly pattern

Be careful not to overdo the room treatment or you'll wind up with a lifeless sound

with the thousands of little irregularities in soft and porous materials, like cloth, wool, fiberglass, foam rubber, etc. When an ordered sound pattern enters this maze, it gets scrambled and rubs against the many surfaces in the maze, causing friction which generates heat and reduces its loudness.

A reflective surface, on the other hand, redirects or scatters sound in several directions, instead of reducing its volume level though absorption. Every great-sounding room is a combination of both absorptive and reflective surfaces. Too much absorption and the music will sound dead. Too many reflective surfaces and the music sounds overly live and bright. Like most things in life, we want the perfect blend.

Couches, over-stuffed chairs, throw pillows all work wonders in rooms

Placing Your Furniture

Now that you understand what the various types of furniture provide in terms of sonics, you can use their qualities to your best advantage.

In an overly dampened room with too many absorptive pieces, you can selectively add hard reflecting surfaces to balance the sound: pictures, wooden bookshelves, tables, and even large vases.

If faced with the opposite problem, where the room is too reflective and needs to be tamed with absorption, adding more soft objects can help: pillows, soft cloth chairs, beanbags, folded blankets, and throw rugs.

Of course, these are but a few of the techniques we can employ to marry in a harmonious relationship our room and speakers. I cover more techniques for room taming in the Advanced Tuning section.

Choosing the Correct Speakers

In your quest to build a great two-channel audio system, you may already own a pair of speakers, or perhaps you're saving up to buy the perfect set. That's a good starting point. For this chapter, however, I am going to assume you're starting from scratch and will provide guidance with that in mind. Even if you have some audio equipment already, I strongly suggest that you at least skim the following paragraphs, to make sure we're on the same page when it comes to the importance of the loudspeaker.

TWO SCHOOLS OF THOUGHT

One of the all-time great rip-snortin', fist-poundin', hair-pullin', teeth-gnashin' debates amongst audiophiles is whether the beginning or the end of the audio chain is the most important. This may sound somewhat academic—even trivial—but I assure you it's a big deal: the ramifications will not only affect your system's performance but will also have a major impact on how you budget for each component.

The debate comes down to a chicken-or-the-egg problem that goes something like this. The source-first crowd reasons that the source of the music, whether vinyl or digital, is the single most important element in the system because if you cannot get the information off the disc in the first place, the rest of the chain doesn't much matter. The speaker-first crowd agrees about the importance of a quality music source, but argues that even if perfect information is retrieved from the disc, the quality of that information doesn't matter if the loudspeakers cannot faithfully reproduce it.

If you are on a budget, you will need to choose where to place the greatest percentage of your investment: in the

Is it more important to perfectly capture everything on the source or the quality of reproducing whatever you do retrieve?

source, the middle of the amplification chain, or in the loud-speakers.

For Me, the Answer's Clear

Loudspeakers should take priority, in my view, and here's why. Of all the components in a two-channel audio chain, including turntables, CD players, amplifiers, preamplifiers, DACs, wires, and speakers, the single most flawed component is the loudspeaker—and not by a little.

Where an amplifier, CD player, or record-playing component may measure relatively flat frequency response (how evenly the volume of individual tones is reproduced), the flaws in even the world's most expensive speakers are worse by orders of magnitude. In fact, we can measure speaker quality and interaction easily, both in technical and audible terms. Let me give you an example.

If we compare the sound of two CD players playing the same musical track, there will be differences we can hear on a highly resolving system. Perhaps the highs are little muffled, or there's somewhat less bass, or the impact of a drum whack isn't felt quite as much—audible differences that often take a bit of training and guidance to perceive. Compare that with two different loudspeakers. If we place one manufacturer's speakers in the room and listen to a track at a given volume, then replace those speakers with a pair built by another manufacturer, the music each pair delivers will sound so different that the listener will wonder what the hell just happened.

When we use audio measurement equipment to test the audio outputs of products, source and amplification

Speakers measure a magnitude worse than electronics

gear differences are typically measured in tenths of a dB (a dB is a decibel – a standard measurement of loudness that is generally thought to require several increments before a change can be detected) Loudspeakers, even the best loudspeakers, are applauded if their dB deviation is close to 3dB (a 30 X difference).

While this may sound highly technical, at this juncture in our adventure the implications are quite simple. Because loudspeakers sound and perform so differently in every room, they must be chosen to match their environment as well as our tastes. Where one type or even brand of speaker might be great in a medium-sized room for mostly rock and progressive music, it may not make a jazz or classical aficionado happy. Or perhaps the best choice for your application might be a panel speaker, but your better half took one look and pronounced an ultimatum: "over my dead body is that thing going in our home." Thus, when you combine the technical challenges of loudspeakers with their imposing size and room-dominating features, it might help to understand why I firmly believe they are the single most important component in the stereo chain.

Long story short, the proper choice of loudspeaker is far more important than the source. Speakers have more impact on the eventual audio outcome of your system than all the other components in the chain combined.

Speakers Should be Your Biggest Expense

When it comes to budgeting for your system, the relative expenses for each element change based on the category of system you want. If you're assembling a Casual system, expect to spend between 50% and 70% of your budget on

Speakers are the single most flawed equipment in the entire audio chain

"I COULDN'T MAKE MY MIND UP
SO I GOT ONE OF BOTH."

loudspeakers. For a Serious setup, that ratio drops back to 50% for loudspeakers, and if you're going completely Whacked-Out, speakers take their rightful place in the chain, at between 30% to 40% of the budget. The proportions even out for a simple reason: as the system gets better, it can better resolve small differences in every aspect of the chain. Thus, once we cross a quality threshold with loudspeakers they tend to reveal more and more flaws in the preceding electronics chain, making it incumbent to spend more on the quality of electronics until all aspects are evened out.

In most cases, you're going to spend a minimum of half your total expenditure on the very finest loudspeakers you're able to put into your home. With a magical pair of high-performance speakers, you can make music in your home something few have had the pleasure of hearing.

Spend the bulk of your funds on acquiring the best speakers you can afford

The Different Types of Speakers

There is a greater variety of loudspeakers than of any other components in the chain. Where the choices in electronics might be as diverse as transistors vs. tubes, and the choices of phono cartridge feature moving magnets vs. moving coils, speaker types take us down a wild and wacky path which can often numb the mind, palpitate the heart, and enrage the hemorrhoids. There are box speakers, planars, plasmas, ribbons, electrostats, open baffles, closed baffles, panels, horns, sealed, ported, passive radiators, line sources, point sources, one-ways, two-ways, three-ways, four-ways, bipolars, dipolars, transmission lines, actives, passives, in-walls, on-walls, DSPs—not to mention all the hybrids! What's a poor audiophile to do?

Fret not! I am here to help sort out these vexing questions. Together, we're going to take a sensible approach to choosing your loudspeaker, and the first question we're going to answer is what you're hoping for.

Waving the Wand

When I daydream about projects, problems, or new ideas, I often start with the magic wand question: if I had a magic wand, what would I wish for? Forget any restrictions or practical issues. For me, at least, eliminating the nagging problems of reality helps clear my mind of clutter and gets me down to the nitty gritty of what I really want. Perhaps what I want is a small, powerful, and impressive living room setup. That's fine. But maybe what I really want (and might be afraid to even dream about) is a big, ass-kicking, state-of-the-art, high-end audio system that gets me excited just thinking about it. Whatever you're looking for, just daydream

There's perhaps no more crowded and confusing field as speakers

a bit and figure out what you want from the system. From there, we can see how close to possible we can get you.

Hopefully, your dream system has fallen into one of the three categories I've previously mentioned. Yeah? Good, just keep that in mind as we now look at the various types of speaker possibilities.

NARROWING DOWN A COMPLEX FIELD

Though there are hundreds of speaker design ideas, I'm going to break them down into a couple broad groups. Without upsetting too many of my friends in the loudspeaker business (full disclosure: PS Audio also builds speakers), let me stuff a lot of designs into a more manageable list of two speaker types: box speakers and panel speakers. Once you clear away all the marketing cruft and industrial design choices—and ignore the home theater and custom installation market—those two are the most relevant for building a stereo system.

BOX SPEAKERS

Box speakers are the most ubiquitous in today's market. No matter how the designers (and their marketing teams) dress up the box, it is essentially a cabinet containing one or more speaker drivers. At the very beginning of the home-reproduced sound era, music came mainly through a large horn—think of old Gramophones—but it wasn't long before those horns got stuffed into wooden boxes. Those boxes were called consoles or cabinets, and they were often complete systems containing the record player, radio, record storage shelves, amplifier, and speakers. This was the

You'll want to choose your speakers on their colorations and how closely they match your tastes

age of the Hi-Fi Console, and millions of homes had console sound systems.

Fast forward a few decades into the late 1940s and early 1950s and we get the introduction of what came to be known as separates. The guts of the console systems were separated into their component pieces: amplifier, radio tuner, turntable, and a wooden box with a woofer and tweeter. Companies like AR, Klipsch, Altec, JBL, and Magnavox produced large and small wooden boxes stuffed full of woofers and tweeters.

Today, the separate box speaker might look and sound quite different from those of yore, but in principle they are the same. They are commonly referred to as dynamic speakers because, for the most part, they use traditional dynamic driver elements first introduced by pioneers like Jensen, Rice, and Kellogg (no, not the breakfast cereal guys—though sometimes they do snap, crackle, and pop).

The possible advantages of a box speaker are:
- Good bass
- Generally lower cost
- Can play very loud
- Easy for an amplifier to drive
- Full frequency response
- Wide listening area
- Easy setup in the room
- The probable disadvantages of a box speaker are:
- Having to look at big boxes in your home
- Often very heavy
- Dynamic drivers are high-mass and often slow-sounding

Don't be fooled with how different speakers look. Most are all based on the classic box design

PANEL SPEAKERS

Unlike box speakers, panel speakers look more like room dividers. As their name implies, they are typically flat rectangular panels with sound coming out of both sides. They are perhaps a few inches thick and can range in size from something close to a modern 40" flat panel television to as tall as one of those Chinese dressing screens or portable room dividers. A typical panel speaker's dimensions might be 29" wide by 70" tall, by 2" thick.

Panel speakers first hit the consumer market back in the early 1950s, with Arthur Jantzen's electrostatic speaker and Peter Walker's well-known Quad electrostatic loudspeaker. In the late 1960s and mid-1970s, panel speakers became popular as companies like Magneplanar entered the scene, as well as Acoustat and later Martin Logan.

What all these products had in common was a lack of boxes, though some, like Martin Logan, combined panels

"I'M PLEASED YOU'VE BOUGHT THE RIGHT SPEAKERS BUT WHAT ABOUT THE LEFT?"

Figuring out what you hope to achieve with your system helps narrow down your choices

and boxes. These tall thin frames produced sound in ways very different than the dynamic drivers and boxes that still dominate the field of speakers today.

The possible advantages of a panel speaker are:

- Excellent high-frequency response
- Excellent transient response
- Amazing clarity
- Not big boxes
- The probable disadvantages of panel speakers are:
- Having to look at giant room dividers
- They often do not play loudly
- They can be tough for amplifiers to drive
- They have limited bass response
- They can be difficult to set up
- Very narrow listening area
- Their frames vibrate

CHOOSING THE RIGHT SPEAKER TYPE

While we audiophiles endlessly bicker over what speakers to buy, most of us opt for box speakers over panels. Why? There are two great reasons: first, because only a select few choose to place large panels into their homes and tolerate their eccentricities, and second, because the thin speaker drivers used in panel speakers can also be placed in boxes—offering many of the same sonic advantages.

I liken those who play with panel speakers to those who lust after vintage automobiles. Sure, they are unique and, in many ways, have some better qualities than what modern manufacturers pass off as cars. For instance, if you like to work under the hood, vintage cars have plenty to

Some of the most transparent sounding systems are based on panel speakers

tinker with: carburetor, distributor, horn, etc. By contrast, modern cars might as well be one giant circuit board. But can I be honest with you? Not many people I know want to dirty their hands fixing old cars. Hell, I drive an electric car that doesn't even have a hood to look under!

My point is simple. If you want great performance without learning a new trade or getting a divorce, you're likely going to want to pass on panel speakers and move straight away into the box variety.

It's not an accident box speakers are the most common style

CHOOSING THE RIGHT BOX SPEAKER

Armed with the knowledge that you're going after a box speaker, it's time to roll up your sleeves and get down in the weeds with choices. You've already identified your dream system, so we'll start with the Casual System first. If you're moving towards the other two categories, feel free to jump ahead.

CASUAL SYSTEM SPEAKER CHOICES

At this level you've budgeted between $1,000 and $5,000 for your system, 50–70% of which should go towards your speakers. That means you're looking to spend $500–700 for an inexpensive setup but no more than $2,500–$3,000.

Now, what are you hoping to achieve? Do you want to build a system that does justice to every kind of music on the planet? Hopefully not, because in this price category we're going to have to pick and choose our focal points. There are no worthwhile speaker systems in this price range that will get spectacular results for everything from a quiet jazz trio to a full symphonic orchestra to properly pounding out Eddie Van Halen or Jimi Hendrix guitar riffs at live levels. That means you're going to have to choose what you will be listening to most.

A second consideration will be the subwoofer. A subwoofer is a separate box with a powered woofer inside. It provides the deep low bass notes that are the fundamental foundations of music. If you'll recall how my wife Terri configured her system, she spent the bulk of her budget on her small KEF LS50s, but she added a REL subwoofer. Together, they formed a full-range system that covers all the frequencies she wanted to capture.

Some speakers have powered subwoofers built in, but most do not, and nearly all of them claim that a subwoofer is unnecessary. While that may be true for a few models of carefully crafted speakers, it's rare that a full-range speaker has adequate low frequency performance. If you can manage to spend the maximum we've allowed for the Casual System, seriously consider adding a subwoofer into your speaker budget (or at a later date as funds permit).

A third and final consideration will be whether to use floor-standing, bookshelf, or stand-mounted speakers. If you were planning on using a small pair of bookshelf speakers that are actually on a bookshelf, or tucked away next to the fireplace, or buried on some table, the Audiophile's Guide is probably not going to be much help to you. While bookshelf speakers sitting on bookshelves can make some nice music, they will never be high-end and certainly will never offer the level of performance we strive to attain within these pages. That narrows the choice to floor-standing or stand-mounted.

There are very few truly full range loudspeakers despite what manufacturers tell you

Stand-mounted speakers are actually bookshelf speakers mounted atop a stand, or any small box speaker sitting on top of a stand. But since they are out in the room, instead of blocked by bookshelves or other debris, we will be able to maneuver them for good imaging and proper tonal balance. A floor-standing loudspeaker, by comparison, is basically a bookshelf speaker with the stand built in. Let me reiterate: a floor-standing loud-speaker is basically a bookshelf speaker with the stand built in. They both take exactly the same amount of floor space, but the floor-standing speaker has a few advantages the stand-mounted version does not. The biggest advantage of building the stand into the box is all the extra room inside the box. That added square footage helps the speaker's woofer produce deeper bass. In the smaller stand-mounted version, the amplifier has to work harder to generate low bass notes, and it never quite sounds as nice as you want (blame the laws of physics).

While you may decide on a stand-mount speaker for some mysterious aesthetic reason, like my wife Terri did, I cannot imagine why. As a fashion-challenged nerdy engineer, I am flummoxed trying to understand why anyone would choose a stand-mount over a floor-mount, unless the speaker had been handed down from your ancestors (and that's not a good reason anyway).

SERIOUS AND WHACKED-OUT SYSTEM SPEAKERS

I am going to group these two categories together because, aside from the budgetary constraints mentioned earlier,

Panel speakers are not for everyone

their goals are pretty much the same. In a Serious System, and certainly in the Whacked-Out version, your mission with speaker choices comes down to one basic idea: don't compromise.

At these levels, you're going to drop a minimum of $10k for the speakers and likely much more. If your pocketbook is squealing at the notion of these big figures, consider the used market. Speakers, like automobiles, drop in value pretty quickly, so you can pick up a great pair of second-hand speakers for a lot less than a new pair might cost. That's the good news. Like everything audio, though, buying used is a double-edged sword. The problem with used speakers is twofold. First, due to the aging of surrounds and pliable materials in the speaker drivers, I'd shy away from anything older than 10 years. Second, you're going to need to know what you want before acquiring a used pair. If you don't like them, it's pretty much impossible to audition and return a previously owned set of speakers. That said, if you brave the used speaker market, you can typically get twice the speaker for half the price of new.

In the Casual category I mentioned two decision points: whether or not to add a subwoofer, and whether to use a stand-mount or floor-standing speaker. These two questions should mostly be settled when you get to the more serious setups: a stereo subwoofer pair is a must, and seriously, why in the world would you compromise with a stand-mounted pair of speakers?! You're going floor mount.

For this category, you'll also want to pay attention to the types of drivers used, in particular the tweeter and midrange. The very best tweeters and midranges tend to be

Don't compromise on speakers. If you can't afford new ones consider used

the same as used in panel speakers: ribbons and planars, or at least lightweight and low-mass dynamic drivers with extended frequency response well beyond 20kHz.

If you're going with a box speaker it is likely going to be a three-way or even a four-way design, with most being in the three-way camp. This means the frequencies are divided amongst three driver types: woofer, midrange, and tweeter. Here, the quality of the frequency-dividing network between the driver components (the crossover) matters greatly. Do your research and learn about the designer's choices in components: film and foil capacitors, air core and copper foil inductors, audio-grade resistors, and OFC wiring arc good examples of what you want to see.

For the woofers, demand as full range as you can get—30Hz to 20Hz on the low end is quite good. However, no matter how full a range they measure, you're still going to need a proper subwoofer pair—a prerequisite for a Serious and above system. Subwoofers add that finishing touch of reality to a high-performance stereo. While some people argue that good subs are unnecessary because music doesn't contain much content below 41Hz—the E string on a double bass or piano—they either misunderstand the subwoofer's purpose or don't listen to pipe organs where pedal C-1 rumbles below human hearing at 8Hz. We'll discuss subwoofers in greater detail in a later chapter.

Lastly, while it may be tempting to go with self-amplified and digitally corrected loudspeakers, I would urge you to think long and hard before going that route. A lot of good work has taken place in these areas but, as of this writing, a passive loudspeaker is still your best bet. Relying on

Small stand mounted speakers take up the same amount of floor space as do floor standing speakers

external separate power amplification has the advantage of tailoring the amp and speaker together for best synergy.

I cannot emphasize enough the importance of the loudspeaker. This is a make or break decision, so take your time, reach out to those you trust, and do not compromise.

What Company's Speaker to Go With

Take the time to find out what the company's goals and aspirations are

By the time this Guide is published, my company PS Audio will be making a line of great loudspeakers—which makes your choice simple. Buy ours! Alright, alright, I'll stop the shameless plug. Truth is, there are a few great speaker companies to choose from, but—and this is where it gets tough—the speakers you don't want far outnumber the ones worth your precious dollars. Sad but true. The vast majority of loudspeakers may be technically within your budget, but most of them are not going to make you happy. So how do you choose?

My advice is rather straightforward: choose the company, its people, and its mission—not just the speaker. Look, in every field there are surprising miracles, lottery winners, overnight stars, and shocking discoveries. But for the most part, it's the tried and true, the steady-as-she-goes success stories that you'll want to fall back on. And I do not mean choosing a company just because they've been around since your dad was still learning to tie his shoelaces. Plenty of products you may not be interested in are made by old companies, clinging to what used to work. No, what I want you to do is a little homework to see if your values line up with theirs. Once you find a company you're comfortable with, a company whose mission matches your own, that's when it's time to check their references, see what kind of reviews they get, and learn what people think about them. But first, you need to see if you two share the same goals.

Take for example vaunted longstanding companies like JBL, Bose, Sonos, and Klipsch. All four companies make great and well-respected speakers for some portions of the market. But while their outer personas speak of quality and music, look deeper at their stated claims. JBL mostly serves the pro market with sound-reinforcing speakers for live events—but you're interested in home audio. Bose is heavy into the consumer market and strives to give good average sound for the dollar, but is that what we're trying to do here? Sonos is the leader in connected home audio, but few believe they strive for audiophile quality performance, and Klipsch—while once dedicated to bringing the sound of live music into your home—is now on a different sort of mission. This is from their website:

> *"Delivering an intense sound experience in an elegant package, Klipsch floor standing speakers provide soaring highs and booming lows while complementing your home décor."*

See what I mean? While soaring highs and booming lows might interest many, they are not what *you* are looking for, not if you're an audiophile. Audiophiles are looking for honesty, purity, and full-range excellence that brings the sound of live musicians into the room without coloration or affectation. If purity of music—bringing the truth and life of what's recorded on the disc—is what a company is

Some of the biggest names in the industry make some pretty mediocre sounding products

aiming for, then they have a fighting chance to earn your business.

Lastly, make sure you can take home your choice of loudspeaker and play with it in your living space. The fact it might sound good at your friend's house, or in a dealer's showroom, or using the setup of a reviewer, is perhaps helpful, but in the end, it must work in your home and offer you what you're hoping for.

Choosing the Correct Electronics

A lot of the advice I gave you in the last chapter (on choosing the right speakers) also applies to choosing the right electronics. Here too, you'll want to consider the company, its people, and its mission, not just the individual products. Keep in mind, though, that despite similar measurements and the opinions of some experts, different companies' electronics sound very different from each other. A phono preamplifier or power amplifier from my company, PS Audio, will absolutely sound different in your system than similar equipment from another company, at least if you follow the Guide when selecting and setting up your speakers. Without reservation, I can tell you that any resolving, high-performance, two-channel audio system will quite easily uncover significant sonic differences between electronics and even between cables—but we'll save that particular headache for a later chapter.

Your biggest challenge is not choosing a company to patronize but determining just what you're going to need. And here's where it gets a little dicey. I've advised a lot of people on building high-end stereos, but I haven't a clue whether you, dear reader, are putting together your first two-channel setup or if you have 30 years of experience and a room full of carefully curated electronics. So, as before, I'm going to start from the beginning and trust that more experienced readers will skim the intros and move right to the meat of the chapter (or, as we vegetarians might prefer, the artichoke-heart of the matter).

GOING TO THE SOURCE
Perhaps the first question any of us—expert and newbie

Electronics all sound different. The degree of difference depends greatly on the resolution of your system

alike—should be asking is this: what's your main source of music? Here, vinyl and digital are really the only two viable options, but nearly everyone with a strong preference can also accommodate the other format. Vinylphiles will likely have a token streaming or CD source in their systems, and vice versa. That's fine, but just like some speakers can better reproduce certain types of music, it's important to decide where your main focus will be.

If you'll indulge me, I'd like to take a few minutes to explain why this choice is critical. Vinyl and digital are very different sounding mediums, so each reproduction system will eventually have to make compromises to properly support either. Records are dynamically restricted relative to digital, meaning most vinyl discs are mastered differently, so they sound different than a digital track of the same song—which isn't to imply vinyl's inferior (it is not), just that it is different. Few if any systems handle both mediums perfectly, so don't expect yours to do so either. Many audiophiles have strong (and often wrong-headed) opinions on which medium sounds better, but they tend to judge quality based on a system instead of the mediums at the heart of that system.

Let me give you an example. My good friend and veteran audio reviewer, Michael Fremer of Stereophile Magazine and The Analog Planet, is the de facto emperor of vinyl. Michael knows more about vinyl and its playback than perhaps any 10 experts in the world combined. His system is amazing, and yes, vinyl always sounds better at his home than it does on our own reference system. But at the same time, digital playback is clearly inferior

There's no one perfect medium. Both digital and analog can provide a wonderfully musical experience

on his system. Michael has spent a lifetime tweaking and honing his amazing system for one task and one task alone: the perfection of vinyl playback. He often throws together a well-respected digital add-on and makes a comparison. The point here is simple. Vinyl and digital each have their strengths and weakness. Optimizing your playback system for one or the other is the smartest thing you can do.

ANALOG-BASED SYSTEMS

From as long ago as 1877, when Thomas Edison first introduced the Gramophone, through Sony & Philips' 1982 introduction of the Compact Disc, scraping a needle through the grooves of a record (or passing a roll of magnetic tape across a tape deck's playback head) was the exclusive basis for playing back music in the home. Over that long century of playback, and after the era of tape recorders passed, engineers and Hi-Fi buffs have perfected the analog vinyl playback system so that today, records are one of the best-sounding mediums ever to grace our homes.

Vinyl sounds terrific but be careful. It can be expensive and it's hardly hassle free

If you've never had the experience of hearing a great vinyl playback system for yourself, I must tell you that you are missing something. I cut my teeth on vinyl and there's forever a soft spot in my heart for the drop of the needle, the ticks and pops one hears before the music begins to play, and the sheer rich musicality of a proper vinyl system. It can be heaven on Earth.

That's the good news. The bad news is that vinyl playback can also be a royal pain in the ass: cleaning records, washing records, using an anti-static zapper, cartridges wearing out, dust on the needle, grandkids bending back a $2,000 diamond stylus connected to a boron cantilever, having to get off the couch and flip the record over, VTA, cartridge alignment, loading requirements...the list goes on. Still, once properly set up, a good analog system can be pure blissful magic.

If you're going to base your system around vinyl, then the electronics and hardware are going to be especially critical. This is really difficult on the Casual System budget, because a good vinyl-based system can be quite expensive. You not only have to get the right cartridge, arm, and turntable combo, but then you're going to need a proper phono preamplifier—and all of that before you get to the preamplifier, power amplifier, and speakers that makes it all work. We'll get to the specifics shortly, but let me say up front that for those on a limited budget, you're really going to have to compromise, but that doesn't mean forever.

You see, sometimes a great budget audio system comes together in stages. You can start with a meager setup with but one or two prized possessions—keepers, if you will—then, as you save up enough money, upgrade some of the compromised bits. So, let's begin there. Below, I have listed critical components for any system. Plan to invest well in those pieces, but don't worry if you need to postpone other upgrades until later.

Here's my must-have list. For a medium to higher-end Casual System, plan to spend more on the first two items than the last two. If you're working with a lower budget, see the later section on integrated parts, receivers, and separates.

Knowing whether you want to focus on analog or digital will be a big help

- Phono preamplifier
- Phono cartridge
- Arm
- Table

And yes, I did just feel a great disturbance in the force. It's okay. After writing more than 3,000 daily blog posts, 1,000 daily YouTube videos, and literally hundreds of thousands of emails (probably approaching 1,000,000), I am used to the hoots and howls of disagreement.

As with loud speakers, if you're going with vinyl don't skimp on the budget

For the record, yes, I am an electronics designer and manufacturer and no, my company does not make phono cartridges, arms, or tables. But the order of my list is only a little self-serving. Back in PS Audio's infancy, in 1974, our only product was a phono preamplifier. Back then, every preamplifier on the market included an integrated phono preamplifier. There were almost no separate phono preamplifiers at all until we launched ours. We designed and built a separate device because we realized the importance of this critical piece of gear, and focusing all our design efforts on this one task yielded extraordinary sound.

A phono preamplifier takes the tiniest of signals from the phono cartridge (itself little more than a couple of magnets and coils of wire) and performs what some believe to be a minor miracle. Without the addition of much noise (hiss) the extremely tiny signals are amplified at least 1,000 (and up to 30,000) times, passed through a type of bass and treble control called an RIAA curve, and output on the other end (hopefully) without distortion, noise, or modification to the original wiggles of the record groove.

"I TOLD YOU MY TURNTABLE SYSTEM WASN'T TOO BIG."

This is an amazing feat of engineering, one which has a huge impact on sound quality. Think of the phono preamplifier as the bedrock of your vinyl system. This is where you invest your funds first; it's not the place to compromise.

Phono cartridges are mechanical devices that we often select for their sonic colorations. They're fragile, prone to replacement from time to time, and work synergistically with the arm and table. You'll find that over time, these will be the elements you'll need to continually adjust, tweak, replace, and fret over (especially if you have inquisitive children flitting about). All this is much easier to deal with and optimize if you have a solid bedrock in your phono preamplifier: a sonic anchor for the system, one that can test the mettle and performance of more transitory elements like cartridges, arms, and tables.

It's alright to invest heavily in your core audio products while going on the cheap for everything else until funds allow

Don't be afraid to go as financially deep as you need to with the phono preamplifier. I'd much prefer to see you get an awesome phono preamplifier and settle for a midrange arm, table, and cartridge. Over time, it's easy enough to upgrade the mechanics, and you'll be much happier than if you skimp on the preamp.

Trust me.

A great phono preamp is the heart of the vinyl based system

DIGITAL-BASED SYSTEMS

In the early days of digital audio, back in the 1980s, CDs were touted by Sony as "Perfect Sound Forever."

Bullshit.

Man, those early CDs and players were nothing short of dreadful. Still, for the most part, early attempts at getting consumers to replace their vinyl libraries with the new-fangled silver discs were quite successful. Sony had two main goals: craft a lower cost way of printing discs (CDs are cheap to make; vinyl's expensive) and resell the millions of releases once again, thus raking in enormous profits. As CDs were being launched, Sony Entertainment was busy buying up record labels like RCA, Columbia, Epic, Arista, and Ariola, among others.

Everything went great for Sony, such that by the early 2000s pundits were attending mock funerals for vinyl records, gleefully proclaiming "Vinyl is dead!" But we audiophiles had neither quit our vinyl nor agreed that digital was better, let alone "good." We recognized just how God-awful these early players and discs sounded. Some companies, including PS Audio, realized the potential of digital audio and committed themselves to making it listenable (and eventually, amazing). A handful of manufacturers (including the big boys Sony, Yamaha, Philips, etc.) kept working on the promise of digital until many considered it the superior format. But that didn't happen overnight.

Building a state-of-the-art digital system is less costly and easier than building a vinyl system of the same quality. If you're just starting out and have yet to decide which way to go, I would nudge you towards digital, if for no other reason than it's easier to get started and make great music out of the chute. Indeed, a proper digital-based system, whether streaming, hard drive-based, or CD-based, can be a revelatory audio experience. At PS Audio, our Music Room Two Reference system is digital-based, and we routinely set folks back on their heels with how natural and lifelike the music sounds. Many have walked out of that room shaking their heads, proclaiming that they have never heard anything close.

For digital systems, I recommend two critical components. First, invest relatively heavily in a Digital to Analog Converter (DAC). Then, focus on a source—CDs, a hard drive, a server, a streaming service, and so on. (For low-end budgets, see the later discussion on integrated parts, receivers, and separates.) Over time and as your budget allows, you can replace the weaklings in the group and get substantial improvements without suffering through bad sound in the meantime.

Unlike my list in the vinyl section, I don't expect much controversy about these priorities. Most audiophiles agree that the DAC is the key element to a successful two-channel digital-based system and that the sources—CDs, hard drive, server, streaming—are less vital. The DAC's function is to take digital audio—the binary computer language

A digital based system is by far the easiest to assemble and operate

of 1s and 0s—and convert them into something we analog-based humans can recognize as music. Computers run on bits, but humans need analog sounds. The conversion of these bits into the analog of what we perceive as sound is a critical element. As in the vinyl system, this one piece of kit becomes the bedrock of your stereo.

The performance of a DAC can be measured only up to a point. We do not understand all the fine nuance and mechanisms of the ear/brain response system well enough to choose a DAC on measurements alone. Like just about everything in high-end audio, you will need to audition various DACs to find which one will have the greatest synergy in the system. A cutting-edge DAC with razor-sharp etched detail isn't going to sonically play nice with a similar sounding amplification and loudspeaker chain. The results could be ear-splitting, or at best fatiguing over time. Like cooking and wine tasting, assembling a two-channel audio setup has to involve the proper blend of components from companies you trust.

The Digital to Analog Converter is the heart of the digital audio system

VACUUM TUBES VS. SOLID-STATE

Once you've decided which source to focus your attention on, the next challenge will be to decide between the two main avenues of amplification, vacuum tubes or solid-state.

For those new to this field, the idea of vacuum tubes might sound antiquated or even absurd. Vacuum tubes were what my parents listened to—and I am 72 years old! Engineers, I can almost hear the hairs rising on the back of your necks, so let me reassure you: not all amplification devices sound the same. Tubes, BJTs (Bipolar Junction Transistors), JFETs (Junction Field Effect Transistors),

and MOSFETs (Metal Oxide Semiconductor Field Effect Transistors), all have distinct sounds, even if the circuits they occupy measure the same.

To make a gross generalization, when listening to circuits based on tubes, we can use words like warm, rich, fat, and lush to describe their sound. When listening to BJT circuits, we can use words like detailed, precise, extended highs, and etched to describe how music is presented. As for the FET series, they tend to be closer to tubes though seasoned with BJT properties. Now, these characteristics are all very much dependent on where in the circuit they are employed, as well as how the designer has implemented them (which is yet another reason to select your equipment based on the aims and aspirations of the company and the designer, rather than on the reviews or the sales pitch).

The audible differences between tubes and transistors have narrowed over the years

Generally speaking, tube-based circuits are more expensive than any of the other choices, so those on tight budgets might do well to stick to their solid-state choices. Further, tubes of the same type all sound different. A 12AX7 vacuum tube from one manufacturer will likely sound quite different than that from another vendor. Audiophiles routinely "tube-roll," meaning they will swap out the same kinds of tubes from different manufacturers, to tailor the sound to their liking. And, tubes die over time and must be replaced, while solid-state devices generally stay stable.

Tubes have more than just a sense of enhanced sweetness to them

For those on the Casual System, I recommend sticking with solid-state. Though I love the sound of vacuum tubes and PS Audio makes quite a few products whose inputs are based on vacuum tubes, I also have a major practical streak running through me. It was born of many, many decades of being in financial hardship and having to make do with what I had on hand.

Preamplifiers and Power Amplifiers

A two-channel stereo system is very much like a chain: its strength and vitality are measured by the links that compose it. The musical signal must pass through each part of the chain before it arrives at your ear. I continually harp on the idea that it all matters, that every element within the signal path affects the final outcome. While that's true, some parts play a more important role than others. As mentioned earlier, the loudspeakers play the most important part in reproducing music, and close behind are the sources of that music, whether vinyl or digital. Not far behind sources are the control and power amplification equipment.

When writing this tome, I greatly struggled with the decision to place preamps and amps in third place along the chain. They're so important to the final outcome that it breaks my heart to choose sides like this, but when there are budget constraints, and somehow it seems there are always budget constraints, one has to pick and choose.

The job of a preamplifier is to select the source input and control the volume. It's the control center of our world and as such, it plays a critical role in the chain. For it is here where all the work we've invested in our source-bedrock can be lost. Fortunately, there are more good preamplifiers than good sources. Preamps, from a design perspective, are relatively simple, so with a bit of due diligence and care, you can land a really good one for your system.

The job of a power amplifier is to be married to the loudspeaker. This is a romance that can go both ways: cooperating or acting as a logjam for everything that has come before. The power amp takes the medium-sized signal from the preamplifier and converts it to a much larger signal, then does a bit of trickery to convert that signal to power (as expressed in watts). For reference, one horsepower is the equivalent of 745.7 watts. Why do we need a fraction of a horsepower for our speaker? Because like automobiles, speakers too have motors. This motor is somewhat like the one in my Tesla: it's an electric motor generally consisting of a coil of wire and a magnet (for standard dynamic speakers).

Preamps and power amps play a vital role in the reproduction of music

As in a car, the quality and quantity of those watts matter greatly. If your power amplifier is underrated for the job of driving your speaker, you're going to be unhappy.

"YOU CAN NEVER HAVE
TOO MUCH POWER."

*It is a common
myth that too
powerful of an
amplifier is to be
avoided*

Underrated amps can cause a loss of dynamic range, a squeezing of the sound, distortion, and clipping (a distortion that at its worst can actually damage your loudspeaker). It's almost never a problem to have too many watts, yet almost always a bad situation to have too few. For example, one of our amplifiers is a 1200-watt monoblock with a vacuum tube on its input. This is a wonderful sounding amplifier, with far more watts than any loudspeaker's likely to use, but we recommend it for nearly every loudspeaker regardless of that loudspeaker's power rating.

When you play your music at a certain volume level, you see, the wattage needed to reach that volume is identical regardless of what amplifier is connected. In other words, if it takes 25 watts to drive your speaker to a reasonably loud listening level for a given audio track, every amplifier of any type will deliver that same wattage to attain that same loudness. Thus, our 1200-watt amplifier will only output the necessary 25 watts in response to a given volume setting on the pre-amplifier, just like a 100-watt (maximum) amp would.

The reason people are encouraged to purchase as many quality watts as they can afford is something called headroom. It works the same way in cars. A Ferrari and a Ford Pinto need the same horsepower to move an identical weight at a certain speed. The difference is that the Ferrari's engine is loafing—just purring along and ready for that touch of the gas pedal to leap forward on command—while the Pinto may be struggling near its limits just to move the car, with little energy in reserve to get out of its own way when you floor it.

INTEGRATED PARTS, RECEIVERS, AND SEPARATES

Given enough resources, you always want to choose separates for your amplification and source chain. But when building a low-budget system, that option won't always be available. Separates are more expensive, and you also run the risk of mismatching equipment or having to buy extra interconnecting cables. To avoid those issues, one option is using an integrated amplifier to suit all your needs. For example, PS Audio's Sprout integrated amp combines a phono preamplifier, pream-plifier, DAC, internet streamer, and a power amplifier, all in one small and affordable chassis. It's the perfect piece of equipment if you're building a $1,000 budget system (including speakers). That's exactly what Terri and I enjoy in our home.

The power amplifier is often the most ignored component in the chain, yet its role is critical

The downside to an integrated part is that none of the individual systems are as good as a separate version, which is why I always point people towards separates. But if you are on a limited budget, consider one of the excellent integrated amplifiers available from a decent handful of worthwhile companies that work hard at making music. They're often the best choice for two-channel newbies and they offer an easy upgrade path along the way.

There are some great high performance integrateds on the market today

Receivers are integrated amplifiers that add a whole bunch of features, mostly bells and whistles you neither need nor want. Stay away from them: the more stuff designers cram into a single box, the worse the unit sounds. As an engineer who has designed my fair share of equipment, I can tell you that it's damned hard to design a great integrated system and nearly impossible to add more stuff and maintain quality, honest sound. Stay with integrated parts (or just buy separates) and avoid receivers.

Whichever electronics you choose, make sure you can take home your choice of amplification or source equipment and play with it in your living space. If the company doesn't allow this, move on to a competitor that has enough confidence in their products to withstand your test. It might sound good at your friend's house, or in a dealer's showroom, or on a reviewer's setup, but in the end, it must work in your home and help you meet your audio goals.

Basic Setup

By this point you've decided on speakers, electronics, and where to put them all. So it's time to roll up your sleeves and get started making some music. While any room in the home can be turned into a great listening room, the most common choice is the living room, so that's what I'll be referring to when I mention a room. If you have other plans, the same concepts will apply, so no worries.

Most people have no idea how three dimensional a stereo system can sound

WRANGLING 3D SOUND FROM TWO SPEAKERS

It might seem like a crazy idea to recreate three dimensions from two speakers. After all, how in the world do a pair of speakers produce depth, height, width, and specific image placement? In fact, when we have everything just right, the sound should not appear to come from the two speakers at all. Instead, all the music should be completely detached from the two speakers and present itself behind them, as if the performers were standing there. How is that possible?

This neat magic trick takes advantage of our stereo hearing. Our ears do a heck of a lot more than just listening. Each ear is constantly measuring and comparing all sorts of things like timing, relative loudness, angle of approach, and phase relationships. Just as our two eyes each see a slightly different image, which is then assembled in our brains as a three-dimensional picture that includes depth and spatial information, so too our separated ears perform the same sort of function.

If you have a moment, close your eyes and just listen to your surroundings. As soon as the visual noise dies away your hearing will become more sensitive, and you'll begin to gauge your surroundings with only your ears. You can easily tell where sounds emanate from, how close objects are to you, and even how big they might be. Still, one of the great questions I often get is how it's possible for music to seem to come from behind the loudspeaker. Intellectually, we understand the speakers broadcast out of the speaker's front, but if we do our job right it shouldn't sound like that.

Here's an easy way to imagine what is happening. Picture in your living room a trio of musicians, perhaps a standup bass player, a singer, and an acoustic guitarist. The three occupy the space behind your loudspeakers. You wish to record them and play the sound back later, so just imagine your speakers have morphed into microphones. You point each of the two microphones away from you and at the performers, then press record on your machine. Once the musicians are gone and you wish to recreate their performance, you reverse the process and point the speaker-mikes back at the listener. If we've done a good job, the speakers should perfectly reproduce what the microphones recorded, including space, depth, and placement.

In the following paragraphs and chapters, I will help you attain this most magical of events in your own home, making your speakers all but disappear.

WHERE TO PLACE YOUR SPEAKERS

We will start with speaker placement in the room because there's nothing more important than where your speakers sit. There are tons of opinions about where to place speakers for best performance. In a rectangular room, for example, you have to decide between the long wall and the short wall. In a square room there are different considerations, and then there are rooms open on several sides such that we have neither rectangle nor square.

To the average listener, stereo is a flat and two dimensional experience. This guide will help dispel that notion

The easiest way to approach this problem is to place the speakers where you're most comfortable having them. In a professional showroom, you can bring carpenters in to make changes, but homes need to be lived in and enjoyed. So, here are a few ground rules to get started.

- Speakers need to be away from the wall. If you're hoping for your speakers to disappear, you'll need some distance between them and the wall behind them, to make room for your imaginary musicians to perform.
- Your left speaker, right speaker, and listening area should roughly form a right triangle. If your left and right speakers are 10 feet apart from each other, your listening area's going to be just slightly less than that. Let's call it 8 feet away.
- Avoid placing large objects between the speakers. One of the worst things you can do is place equipment, fireplaces, furniture, or any large obstructing object between the left and right speakers. If circumstances dictate you haven't a choice, make sure what objects are between the speakers are as low to the floor as possible. Ideally you want the electronics off to the side, where they're convenient to access.

Keep the electronics near your listening are if at all possible

WHERE TO PLACE YOUR ELECTRONICS

As mentioned in the last section, you should avoid cluttering up the space between the speakers, where the three-dimensional image is going to appear. If you want to have a few power amplifiers between the speakers on the floor, that's just fine, but do resist the temptation to stack your electronics high between the speakers. Instead, put them somewhere convenient and accessible.

This, of course, means having to deal with a long set of interconnects between your preamplifier and power amplifier (if you've split the system), or using a long set of speaker cables if all the electronics are together. I've built many systems both ways and while each can work, my preference remains long interconnects and short speaker cables, if that's a practical solution for you.

WHERE TO PLACE YOUR LISTENING SEAT

I wish it were as easy as saying "here's where to place your listening seat," but this turns out not to be quite so simple. For many years, I followed the setup procedure for speaker and seating placement that has become known as the Rule of Thirds. This guideline for speaker setup was originally suggested to me by the late Harry Pearson, publisher of Absolute Sound Magazine. HP, as he liked to be called in print, always assumed people had dedicated listening rooms of decent proportions. He would advise them to place the speakers 1/3 the way into the room from one wall, then place the listening chair 1/3 the way into the room from the opposite wall.

This determined the starting point from which speakers and seating positioned would be moved back and forth in a sort of dance, to get everything to sing properly. I've set up any number of great-sounding systems using the Rule of Thirds. But, over the years, I have come to prefer a simplified alternate technique practiced by a few advanced audiophiles, including my good friend and the owner of

Where your listening seat winds up is more a function of the room than choice

REL subwoofers, John Hunter. From here on out, we'll be using my modified version of this method, which I call IAATB (It's All About That Bass).

Preparing for IAATB

Setting up the system shouldn't take you more than a good Saturday afternoon, but if you can manage it, block off the entire day.

If we're working in the living room it's best to clear away as much space as you can, to give yourself a clear path between the speakers and where you think the listening area will be. Big objects like bookcases, shelving, and plants can stay if moving them would cause World War III (or at least evoke The Glare), but clear away what you can. As for tools, you don't need many: a tape measure, a roll of (easily removable) blue painter's trim tape, a small handheld mirror, and if at all possible, an assistant.

Setting Up Your Grid

To make life easy, set up a grid to help you place the speakers and your listening chair or sofa. It's simple. Once you've cleared the room, locate its center with the tape measure, then run a vertical strip of blue tape down the entire length of the room, so as to denote the center between the left and right speaker. If you have an oddly shaped room, don't stress too much—just give it your best shot. It's not written in stone and for the moment it's only a reference.

First, decide how much space you're willing to put between the speakers and the wall behind them (called the front wall). Four feet is a good minimum, but don't

It only takes a few minutes to set up your grid

go farther than 1/3 the length of the room. We will be adjusting this later, in any case. Starting from the line of demarcation away from the front wall, place a 12–15-foot horizontal length of blue tape (the X axis) to form a T with the vertically-placed center tape (the Y axis).

Second, measure 5.5 feet in each direction off the center line (Y axis) and place another piece of blue tape on the horizontal tape (X axis) that you used to mark the distance from the front wall. This marks the spot where you will place the outer edge of each loudspeaker. Face the loudspeaker so it points towards your listening spot. What you've now done is separate the left and right speakers by approximately 10 feet, from tweeter to tweeter. This is just a starting point.

Third, from the T-junction of where the center line meets the front wall tape, measure 8 feet away from where the speakers will go and stick another piece of tape at that junction, forming yet another X-axis T. This is where your listening spot will be, but don't put a chair or couch there quite yet.

Place your speakers as directed, set up your electronics wherever they will live, connect everything together, and make sure you can play music. Testing with a CD (or streamer) would be easiest—if you do not have a CD player as part of your rig, just pick up a cheap one at Target, Walmart, or Amazon. Most CD/DVD/Blu-ray players should run you less than $50, and it might be nice to have one around for later setup activities. You can also use your turntable: repeating configuration tracks will be a bit more of a pain, but certainly manageable if that's what you prefer. You're also going to need a CD, download, or vinyl

With the Reference Music disc from PS Audio, it's easiest to use the SACD version to put it on repeat

album to play. We offer a great setup disc from Octave Records, The Audiophile Guide's Reference Music disc, available at www.psaudio.com, or you can use your own if you prefer. I am going to assume you're all in and selected the Guide setup disc (it's worth it).

You can order directly from PS Audio as a disc or download

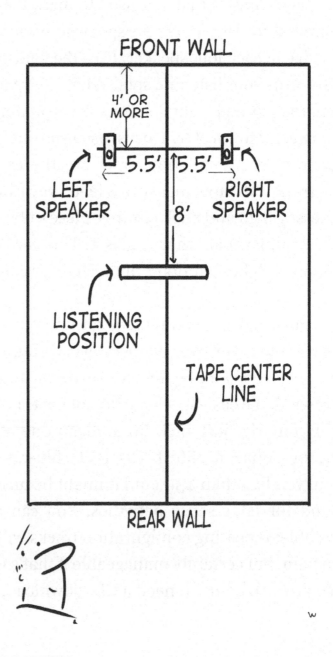

Tuning Your System to the Room

I f your eventual goal is to get the speakers to disappear so that the musicians magically appear as if they were playing live, then step one in the tuning process—finding where you're going to sit—might seem counterintuitive. After all, shouldn't we be focused on dialing in the loudspeakers first? But determining your seating position is actually a critical step, and here's why: our rooms are not friendly to bass notes.

Using bass as the first setup instrument may be counter intuitive but it works

IT'S ALL ABOUT THAT BASS (NO TREBLE)

Meghan Trainor has it right: it is all about that bass. In our initial setup phase, we have to determine where bass notes are at their best. Bass frequencies are the most problematic of all the frequencies within the human hearing range, since they involve long wavelengths, often longer than the room itself. Indulge my nerdiness for a bit, so I can walk you through a quick course in bass problems, then we'll move on to solving them.

When a bass note is played, the woofer generating the bass note pressurizes the room at a specific frequency. In an average-sized room, the resulting pressure wave sets up an unwanted event we call a standing wave, which makes for very uneven sound. Even though the initial string pluck of the bass sets up a steady and equal vibration throughout the room, if the wavelength is longer than the room, at some point it butts up against a hard reflective surface like a wall, ceiling, or floor. When that happens, it doubles back on itself to create a new set of unwanted stationary ripples. A good analogy of this is when two opposing streams of river water form a standing wave, the kind of stationary curl that surfers can ride for what seems like forever (lower your pitchforks, physicists: yes, the surfer's wave is technically static, but this isn't technically a physics course, n'est-ce pas?).

Here's another example. If a bass player plucks a low F note that's about 43Hz (in frequency), its resulting pressure wave is about 25 feet long. If your room is less than that, let's imagine 18 feet, how does that work? Well, truth be told, it kind of doesn't—we get those nasty standing waves. And it gets worse: because rooms have four walls, a ceiling, and a floor, those bass pressure waves are not only building up standing waves, but also bouncing around six ways from Sunday. Some waves collide with each other and, depending on whether they are in phase or out of phase (essentially sucking or blowing), they either add more boom or suck out whatever should be there.

As a consequence, throughout the room, there are areas of good bass, no bass, too much bass, and everything in between. These are known as room nodes (nodes and antinodes), and while there are certainly room treatments that can reduce them (we'll get to those in a later chapter), right now our challenge is to identify where in the room they are and find the best spot for bass response.

There are two ways to deal with this bass problem: 1) fix your listening position and move the speakers around, or 2) fix your speakers and move your listening position. In our case, we're putting the speakers as far away from the front wall and into the room as we can—so that later we have enough room behind the speakers to accommodate our "live" musicians—so the obvious and best course of action is to move our seat.

You can always deal with higher frequencies with room tuning. Bass is much more difficult

"THAT'S IT! DON'T MOVE – WE'VE GOT PERFECT SPEAKER PLACEMENT."

*Definitely get yourself
a copy of the
Audiophile Guide's
reference discs*

GETTING INTO POSITION

First, you're going to stand where you put the second piece of tape on the room's center divider. This is our proposed starting point for seat placement. Pull up a temporary chair—a folding metal chair is perfect, since it's easy to move. In your seated position facing the speakers, angle the speakers approximately 10° to 20° in from the center (this is called toe in), so that the right speaker points approximately to the outside edge of your right shoulder and the left speaker points at the outside edge of your left shoulder. I prefer less toe in than most, but we'll fine-tune this later.

If you purchased the Audiophile's Guide Reference Disc, start with Track 1 and make sure your left channel is correct. Then, play Track 2 and confirm the right channel is correct, Track 3 to make sure the center channel is correct, then go on to Tracks 5 and 6 to verify the phase is correct. These are all important to get right before you go any further. Your speaker's phase is controlled by making certain the red + terminal of your power amplifier goes to the + terminal on your speaker, and then that the − is also correct. If they're wrong, none of the other tuning will matter.

Finally, go to Track 7, designated for getting the bass right in the room. On this track, PS Audio loudspeaker designer/engineer, Chris Brunhaver—quite an accomplished bass player—will run up and down the bass scale. Play this track at a decent level, as if the bass instrument were actually playing in the room. Then, put the track on repeat.

If you did not purchase the PS Audio setup disc, shame on you. But I'll forgive you. Find a solo bass album you like, perhaps Rob Wasserman's Duets or Jennifer Warnes' Famous Blue Raincoat, and use it instead. What's important is that there's a good range of bass notes played over and over.

Time to Get Boppin'

First, remove the chair. Next, with the music playing, stand where the temporary seat was located and listen to the bass performance. On our setup disc recording, all the bass notes should be at even loudness, from the lowest to the highest. Where you're standing they probably are not. Perhaps some sound weaker than others. Perhaps when Chris hits that really low note, it hardly comes through at all. No worries. Slowly start walking towards and away from the speakers as you listen. Every few feet, you'll notice a considerable difference in the evenness of the bass notes.

It shouldn't take too long to find the point where the bass is at its smoothest

Your goal will be to identify the one spot along the center line where the bass is the smoothest.

As you slowly walk back and forth from the temporary seating position (home base), you will notice pretty big differences in both the amplitude (loudness) and quality of the bass notes. You might discover that as you move away from the speakers and closer to the rear wall, one spot features the most even sound and best quality of bass plucks. You want evenness, neither too much of any one note nor too little, and in particular, you want to hear the lowest bass notes played. The lowest (deepest) bass frequencies are the hardest to propagate in a room, so when you find that one magical spot along the room's center dividing tape, stop there and ensure the rest of the notes aren't too uneven.

Getting the center channel perfect pays off with major sonic dividends

It's unlikely you'll find the perfect spot, but you can get close in this first rough approximation. Hopefully you find the sweet spot—or at least somewhere pretty good—before the repeating bass line drives you bonkers. Mark that spot with the tape, remove your original seat marker, and place your temporary chair in the new spot. Next, re-aim the speakers. In your new seated position facing the speakers, angle the speakers approximately 10° to 20° in from the center, so that the right speaker points approximately to the outside edge of your right shoulder and the left speaker points at the outside edge of your left shoulder.

It's time now to go to step two, adjusting for that perfect center image.

THE CENTER IMAGE

Of course, there is no third center speaker in a two-channel stereo setup. Still, you should have a very solid,

palpable center image, as if you had that third speaker generating it. This center image is often referred to as the Phantom Channel. Though there is nothing there, your two speakers are capable of creating a very convincing illusion of its presence.

The center channel of a stereo system happens when our ear/brain mechanism hears exactly the same thing at the exact same time. This is, in fact, what happens when sound is played directly at you. That monophonic sound of a voice or instrument reaches both your left and right ears at precisely the same loudness and time. Your ear/brain mechanism measures this and reports, "it's in the center." If that voice or instrument were to move a few feet to the side, its sound waves would first hit the ear closest to it with a slightly louder amplitude,

The center channel image can be too wide or too narrow. Getting the size just right is essential

"I REALIZE YOUR HI-FI'S SOUNDSTAGE ISN'T QUITE RIGHT BUT DID YOU HAVE TO DEPLOY SPECIAL FORCES?"

Sometimes even fractions of an inch of toe in can make a big difference

followed a millisecond later in the more distant ear at a somewhat reduced volume. "Aha!" the ear declares. "The sound must be over there."

Because our two-channel stereo speakers aren't what's moving, we need to make sure we set them up properly, so that when the recording has equal loudness and arrival time on both channels, the ear/brain is fooled into believing something is in the center.

FRONT AND CENTER

On the Audiophile's Guide Reference Disc, go to Track 9 and place it on repeat. If you didn't purchase the disc, find a simple, well-recorded male or female vocal recording. I can recommend Keith Greeninger & Dayan Kai's "Looking for a Home" (Blue Coast Recordings), Diana Krall's "Body and Soul" (Justin Time Records), or any track from Clandestine Amigo's Temporary Circumstances (Octave Records).

Once you have your cut selected, adjust the volume level to mirror how loud an actual person might be in the room. Volume is extremely important. The louder the voice the bigger its apparent image size, and vice versa. Within your room, do your best to keep the level at about what you imagine that same person might actually sound like, if they were playing live in the room.

Put the track on repeat. Sitting in your seat, listen to the voice or voices you've chosen. How precise, how palpable are they in space? Here you want to achieve a few things: a palpable solid center image, a reasonable approximation of proper height (as if the singer is standing), a center image that appears behind the two loudspeakers, and a voice tonal balance that is neither thin nor fat.

MAKING IT PALPABLE

As the singer starts to perform, a solid center image should appear behind the speakers. The size of that voice should approximate what you might expect if the person were performing in the room.

If the overall size is correct yet the voice sounds thin or is too diffuse, you are going to want to pull your speakers closer together, working in 6" increments. Some people like to make 6" hash marks along the X-axis tape, to make it easier to move them in and out. Being a rather unorganized and basically lazy person, I prefer to just grab my trusty tape measure and lock it down to 6 inches. I then use it to measure 6 inches from the inside edge of each speaker cabinet and, mark the tape with my little black Sharpie, then move the speaker over and repeat on the other side. It's quick, it's easy, and it works. Don't forget to re-aim the speakers. In

The phantom center image is just an illusion

your new seated position facing the speakers, angle the speakers approximately 10° to 20° in from the center, so that the right speaker points approximately to the outside edge of your right shoulder and the left speaker points at the outside edge of your left shoulder (we'll refine this later).

Now, listen again. The voice should sound warmer, fatter, and a bit more in the room. This is because the woofers or midbass drivers of your speakers gain better coupling. The closer together speakers are, the "fatter" the midbass gets due to this increased coupling between channels. If you move them too close together, the center image doesn't get much better, but you'll notice that the other instruments crowd into the center space and lose some of their dimensionality. Work on moving the speakers closer together and further apart until you've nailed the correct balance of a tonally accurate voice, with a solid center image, maintaining the maximum distance apart. Don't forget to re-aim the speakers each time you move them.

Capturing Depth

Depth on a soundstage is an interesting phenomenon. On a well-configured system playing a great recording with proper depth, the singer or center instrument should appear well behind the loudspeakers, at the proper height of a standing person, with the accompanying vocalists or instruments spread out in a soundstage that extends beyond the left and right extremes of the speakers. To get there, you must first get your center image dialed in even better than you already have.

First, remove the speaker toe in altogether. You do this by simply aligning both speakers flat against the X-axis

Proper depth can often extend beyond the boundaries of the room

tape you've laid down on the floor. Thus, they will point straight ahead at the wall behind your listening chair. Then, put Track 9 of the Audiophile's Guide Reference Disc back on repeat and listen again. On most systems, the depth of the soundstage will have now increased, so that the performer seems further behind the loudspeakers than before.

You may find that the center image has now lost specificity. This is to be expected, so you're going to have to experiment a bit to gain your bearings. Ultimately you want to recapture the center image specificity and tonal correctness, without losing too much of your newly acquired soundstage depth. Your tools are primarily adjusting toe in and, if needed, again moving the left and right speakers closer together (while exercising caution). You've already gotten the tonal balance dialed in using the midbass coupling method so, if you're going to move the speakers together or apart, make only small, incremental changes. Your primary tool will be toe in. This step is a dance between depth and image specificity, so take your time and maximize both without sacrificing the other.

Once you believe you have the best combination of depth and center image specificity, next play Track 10 of the Audiophile's Guide Reference Disc. Track 10 has good depth and center image specificity built into the recording, but it also has a few more instruments added to widen the soundstage and provide layered depth. You're listening to this track to make sure you haven't narrowed the soundstage too much while trying to get Track 9 right.

Little steps matter. Take your time. Often, fractions of an inch are all that's needed

As depth changes so too will width and the space between performers

"THERE MUST BE A BETTER WAY TO CAPTURE DEPTH."

Alternate between Tracks 9 and 10 until you find the perfect balance of center image specificity, realistic depth, and wide soundstage width.

Don't be concerned if you have almost zero toe in when you're finished. On PS Audio's reference system, for instance, there is only about 1° to 2° of toe in. The proper amount of toe in has much to do with the speaker's design. If the designer paid attention to the speaker's off-axis response (the smoothness of level when the tweeter isn't pointed directly at your ear), you can enjoy wickedly great depth and soundstage width with almost no toe in. If, however, your speaker's designer is less concerned with off-axis smoothness, then you'll need more toe in. This isn't all bad. Some systems require a great deal of toe in to get everything you want, but the downside of too much toe in is often a narrower "sweet spot"—the size of the listening area.

Take your time, making small changes one at a time. If you find a combo that works, take your blue tape and outline the speaker base, so you can get back to where it works if you continue tweaking. By moving between these states, you'll narrow it down to a point you're happy with, both tonally and image-wise.

FINE TUNING DEPTH

Now, put on Track 11 of the Audiophile's Guide Reference Disc. For Tracks 11, 12, and 13, we carefully measured the distance between the singers and the stereo microphone arrangement. Track 11 was recorded at 3 feet, Track 12 at 6 feet, and Track 13 at 9 feet from the microphone. These three tracks are incredibly important aids in your setup. Knowing exactly how far the performers are from the microphone means you can accurately measure the perceived depth offered by your speakers. In other words, on Track 9, it should sound like the two ladies are 3 feet behind the loudspeakers.

Starting with Track 11, set the system volume level so the two performers are at the right image size. Remember, they should sound lifelike: too big and the volume's too high, too small and the volume's too low.

Next, grab your tape measure and blue marking tape. Place a strip of tape on the X-axis of the center line denoting the approximate middle of the speakers. Using your tape measure and tape, mark another X-axis line 3 feet back (behind the speakers, towards the front wall). If your speakers are out into the room by only 4 feet, it's still a good idea to take this step.

If you find something that works, use the blue marking tape to denote the speaker's position

Then, play Track 11 again and mentally line up the position of the two voices and the tape mark behind the speaker. Are you close? Has the illusion of depth worked? If not, you will want to keep the track playing and begin making small adjustments in speaker placement.

- Pulling the speaker pair away from the front wall (closer to the listener) will increase the depth. Do this in one-inch increments until the singers are at the correct depth.
- Move your seating position forward and backward by a few inches to see which position more accurately represents where the singers should appear.
- More or less toe in will change the relative front to back position of the performers.
- Angle the speakers back by placing a CD jewel case under the front edge. This will change the imaging and affect the depth. Add or remove cases as needed. Once you hit the sweet spot for depth, it may be possible to make a more permanent adjustment by using adjustable feet (if your speaker has them) or isolation pucks.

Listen between the tracks and you can hear singers Jessica and Giselle walking back to their new distance marks

Once you've dialed in Track 11, it's time to move on to the other two tracks, 12 and 13. On each additional track, another 3 feet of distance has been added between the singers and the microphone. If you've managed to setup the speakers properly, you should get a greater sense of depth with each track. Now, what may seem counterintuitive is the actual distances involved. If your speakers are only 4 feet from the front wall, how is it possible to get 6 or 9 feet of additional depth as recorded on tracks 10 and 11? The answer's in the definition of what we're doing: creating the illusion of depth. You don't need an actual 9-foot space between the speakers and the front wall in order to sound like there's greater depth. Even the best systems in the world aren't accurate representations of the recorded three-dimensional sound field, but they produce the illusion of increased depth.

THE FINAL TUNING

Track 14 on the Audiophile's Guide Reference Disc captures the proper height, width, depth, and tonality of a small group. After again setting the proper volume for the track, you should experience a palpable image of the musicians playing behind the speakers in their own three-dimensional space.

Distance from the microphone on the recording is what creates the sense of depth

Using your new-found skills for small tweaks in speaker and listening position, make the final dial-in to have all the elements on this track sound as in-the-room as you can.

This setup procedure can be applied and reapplied as needed, both for equipment changes and positional changes. It's good to remember that this is just the basic setup procedure for the system. There's plenty more you can do if you want to push the envelope. Improvements to the room, connecting equipment, and even the sources and types of music all await your new expertise at perfecting the stereo system in your home.

"Music is to the soul what words are to the mind."

Modest Mouse

Notes and Tips on Audio Tuning

The typical pattern of stereo installation is to plop down a pair of speakers where they look good, wire them to the stack of equipment, press play, and then pray it sounds good (better known as Plug-and-Pray). Chances are it will sound just fine, but that's not why you're reading this book.

If you've followed the steps outlined in the last chapter on tuning, there's little doubt in my mind that you've put together a system better than most. That said, we can all benefit from a checklist to review our work. Here's a set of helpful tips and tricks if you haven't yet gotten your system where you want it.

The music should appear to come from behind the speakers and not be attached

IF THE MUSIC IS STILL STUCK IN YOUR SPEAKERS

If the sound comes out of your speakers or, worse, projects in front of them without a decent soundstage behind and to the sides of the system, here are a few things to check.

- Distance from the front wall. If your speaker pair is shoved up against the front wall (the wall behind them), then there's no room for a soundstage to work in the room. You'll need at least four feet of space, as measured from the back of the speaker to the wall. More is better (to a point).
- Wrong kind of music. Not all recordings will work. Poorly recorded pieces with singers too close to the microphones, or the overly compressed recordings endemic to contemporary rock, won't sound very good. Try a few of the demo cuts on the Audiophile's Guide Reference Disc to see what works.
- Too much toe in. Most speakers like to have a little

toe in but not too much. If the tweeters are angled directly at your ears, you may find that the speakers disappear only when there's a center image, then go back to ping-pong stereo at the outer edges. Try a bit less angle to see.

IF THE BASS IS WRONG OR MISSING

Bass notes are the most difficult to get right in any room. It could be that you have a square room (the worst possible dimensions for bass) or that you haven't nailed the seating position as well as you'd hoped.

- Add a subwoofer. Most "full-range" loudspeakers aren't actually full range: rarely do speakers produce bass into the subterranean regions of a room. They might fare alright on the test bench, but in your room, not so much. That's when it's best to tweak your main speaker pair for the best tonal and soundstage performance, then add a subwoofer pair in a different part of the room to get the bass.

- Position a subwoofer for best bass. Many audiophiles set their subwoofers next to or slightly behind their main speakers because that's where it feels right. Worse, when there's only a single subwoofer used, they will center it between the left and right channels. Wrong idea. The easiest way to set up a subwoofer is to use an old trick that is the opposite of our basic audio tuning method. Instead of moving your seat to where the bass is best, do the opposite. Place the subwoofer in your seating position, then walk around the area where the sub is going to live to find where the bass is best. Once you find that

What you're hoping for is realism as if the musicians were in the room

spot, simply mark it with tape, plop the sub down where the tape mark is, and when you sit in your listening seat, voila! Great bass. *As an aside: in the rare instance that you cannot move your seating position for the best bass response, as described in the chapter on tuning, you can use the same principle to place the main speakers. Instead of a subwoofer, place the main speakers where you sit, point them at the front wall, then walk the space where they will eventually reside to find where the bass is best.

It's easiest to use acoustic instruments or human voice to determine proper tonal balance

IF THE TONAL BALANCE IS OFF

Reproducing music on a high-performance audio system isn't just about building a perfect soundstage and reproducing its image in the home. We also need to make sure the instruments and voices sound lifelike.

- If voices and instruments sound too fat or heavy (or too thin or light-sounding). Because modern separates don't have tone controls (we don't really want to use such things because they dirty the sound), we have to actually fix the problem rather than applying an EQ band-aid. The easiest means of controlling midbass, the area between 200Hz and 500Hz—sometimes referred to as the chest or lower regions of voice and instruments—is to either pull apart the loudspeaker pair or push them closer to the front wall (the wall behind the speakers). Even a few inches make quite a difference. When you pull apart the speakers, the woofers couple together less and act more as individuals. But there's a delicate balance between proper imaging and tonal balance. If you can't pull them apart or put them closer together because of imaging problems, try pushing the speakers closer to the front wall.

IF THE IMAGE SIZE IS WRONG

Sometimes we get everything to be tonally correct and image properly behind the loudspeakers, yet something's wrong: the singers sound as big as our room.

Getting the subsonics right can make a huge difference in believability of sound

- Volume level controls image size. What few people realize is that every track, every piece of music, has a proper loudness level. If we play it too loud, the voices and instruments grow large and out of proportion to their proper size, and vice versa. To make matters more interesting, a proper volume setting is completely room-and circumstance-dependent. If you're sitting alone and voices and instruments appear at their proper size for a given volume control setting, that will change if you add more people in the room. Each person acts as an absorber of sound, so a proper level setting for a particular track of music will be correct only in identical circumstances. Change the number of people and the volume setting will need to be adjusted.

"Music is the mediator between the spiritual and the sensual life."

Ludwig Von Beethoven

Life after Basic Tuning

The proper setup of a high-end audio system is often tedious, always requires a good dose of patience, and definitely benefits from a hopeful eye to the future. The first time you get it right, there's a real sense of satisfaction and accomplishment. You've earned something very few have experienced: a stereo system that can sound heavenly enough to send a chill down your spine.

Proper image size is critical to creating a believable three dimensional image

But is that enough? For many, it's actually more than enough—it's beyond where they dared hope they'd be, and that's great. It's why I wrote this book and what I hope to help people achieve. But for some of you—perhaps as many as 20%—it's just the beginning, something that sparks a hopeful flame that may burn for the rest of your days. That's what happened to me and my life's been the better for it.

Perhaps you, dear reader, have now reached your goal and you'll soon put this book on the shelf or pass it along to a friend. Thank you and congratulations. But let me try to convince you to continue our journey into audio bliss.

THERE'S SO MUCH MORE TO DISCOVER

Our basic audio tuning procedure merely scratched the surface of what is possible in a high-end audio system. We could keep talking about the room, synergy between equipment, advanced tuning techniques, choosing the right music, and discovering the best source—all in service of polishing our systems to a deep luster that will set them apart from every other music system in the world. If you wish to continue down this lifelong path, pushing through basic purgatory to enter audio paradise, then the rest of this Audiophile's Guide is going to be your ticket.

It gets very personal from here on out—good thing, too, because as you move forward, you'll be creating not only a great audio system but a personal monument to music and its reproduction, one that embodies your knowledge, experience, and personality. It will be unlike anything anyone else on the planet has built—crafted out of the same clay available to us all, but fashioned with your hands and built for your pleasure. I am excited to share this with you.

FOR THOSE LEAVING US

For those of you leaving us to go play music, drink wine, make love, be generous, and make the world a better place than it is, enjoy yourselves. Thanks for coming along with us for the ride. I hope it helped in your pursuit of music and better sound. It was fun having you on board!

For the rest, those who want to bravely march into the wilds of audiophile wackiness and the never-ending quest for better, I welcome you with open arms. Onward, fellow audiophiles!

If you've managed to get this far in the book, congratulations. Hopefully it was a help to you

"If music be the food of love, play on."

William Shakespeare

How to Listen

You hear with your ears but listen with your brain. While this may seem an academic observation, it has major ramifications when it comes to the art of high-end audio. Good listeners—sometimes called Golden Ears—are *made*, not born. It is only through training that you can become a good listener, capable of discerning small nuances in music's reproduction that will help you build a great audio system.

What we hear as sound is a combination of ear/brain information

When I first began my Hi-Fi journey back in the early 70s, I could only broadly tell differences between equipment and speaker setups: this one had better bass, perhaps the highs extended further through a particular piece of gear, or the midrange felt recessed with the speakers one way and exaggerated the other way. But it was always a struggle identifying the more subtle details that experienced listeners seemed to instantly pick up on. Only through lots of listening and the kind help of Stan Warren, my friend and co-founder of PS Audio, did I eventually get the hang of how to listen.

I have discovered over the years that it is far easier to help newcomers hone their listening skills by pointing out what to listen for, rather than attempting to educate them as to how it should sound. If you know where to focus your attention, it's pretty easy to tell whether a particular area of sound is more or less real, greater or lesser in quantity, or better or worse in quality. This training is even valuable for non-experts, since as you listen to a broader variety of music, you'll quickly find patterns in the reproduction that you like or do not like—getting the music to suit your tastes over a broad range of recordings.

When learning how to listen, it's most helpful to have music you can rely upon. That's one of the reasons I recommend starting with the Audiophile's Guide setup recordings from Octave Records. It's available in CD, high-resolution download, and vinyl formats, and it's been carefully curated to represent what great recordings sound like. We've chosen very specific musical and vocal instruments and microphone techniques to aid in your evaluation of the system, as well as in your training as a listener.

START SIMPLE

One temptation to avoid is to start with an all-encompassing, busy track of music with a lot of instruments and complexities. It's akin to walking into a loud party and trying to pick out a conversation without any frame of reference. So overwhelming is the rush of sensory information that your brain will struggle to make sense of what you're hearing. Save the big crescendos and audio fireworks for the setup finish. Once you've done the work of getting everything right, it's a real hoot—and a well-deserved reward—to rock out to the 1812 Overture, Pink Floyd's Welcome to the Machine, or your favorite raw and gutsy track that lifts the roof off the house. Just...not at first. We want to ease you into the listening experience with simple music, featuring easy-to-understand instruments and voices.

For example, try Track 15 of the Audiophile's Guide setup recording. This track is a beautifully simple piece featuring a close-miked solo acoustic guitar. First, look for the overall sense that a musician is performing in the room. The guitarist should be sitting down, playing a

By simply following the previous basic setup guide, you should have been able to make a significant improvement in sound quality

standard-size acoustic guitar. If the guitar is too big and your viewpoint too close, reduce the volume level. If it's too small or distant-sounding, raise the level until it's not only the proper size but there's an obvious amount of detail in each string pluck. When you're satisfied, zoom a little closer into those details, as if you're changing magnification levels on an acoustic microscope. As each string is plucked, there's the fundamental note followed by the ringing of the string itself. As the string continues to vibrate, make a mental note of how long you can hear it before it fades into obscurity or is masked by the next string pluck. Next, it's time to increase the magnification on your audio microscope by another level. This time, listen for the string's harmonic overtones. These subtle cues are often buried by speakers without a lot of resolving power, muddled by lower-quality electronics and cables, or masked by aggressive power conditioners. On a properly outfitted, highly resolving system, those overtones should ring and then decay at a natural rate until they meld into the background noise of the room. Often, you can dive deeply enough into the music to hear the overtones and noises as they bounce of the walls of the room they were recorded in.

Great listeners are made, not born. Listening is an acquired skill

Your goal is to have as little loss of information as possible: to listen deeply to the recording and its subtle details, such that one string pluck does not mask the long decay of the previous one. Often, you can change electronics or cables to discover something you hadn't heard before in the recording, a new layer of subtle details. This is exciting—and as long as your tweaks don't harm the

"I'VE GROWN ACCUSTOMED TO HER BASS."

musical truth of the other instruments, more information is always the correct path.

MOVE UP TO MEDIUM

Once you get the hang of hearing small differences in simple music, it's time to move up the ladder a bit. Here you still want to keep it simple but you can add more players and look for more cues.

In Track 16 of the Audiophile's Guide setup recording, we introduce a few more instruments and rely on a more distant, room-encompassing miking technique. While in Track 15 the recording microphone was fairly close to the instrument, so as to capture as many of the fine details as possible, using Track 16 you can pull back to take in more of the environment the musicians are playing in. Of

Simple, less cluttered music helps us sort through what's taking place on the recording

course, your first task will be to set the proper level for the room and the recording. Remember to reduce the volume if the instrumentalists are larger than life (and increase it if they're too small), and you'll soon reach the perfect level for this particular piece of music in your room. Then the real fun starts. First, take in the performance as a whole, to get an overall sense of position of each musician relative to the other players. Once you're comfortable, pay particular attention to the quality of the space between musicians. How separate are they? Do some instruments mask the sound of others? When the music gets louder does the image grow, or does it stay put and become overstuffed and congested? When the bass plays, is it heard as a separate instrument or as part of the overall presentation? Can you hear the room? Do you get a sense of its size?

Save the fireworks for after you're comfortable with listening

Your goal here is to perfectly recreate the sound of separate musicians as if you were there when it was recorded. You should have a sense of the room it was recorded in; the playing of one instrument should not affect or mask the sound of another. Likewise, when the group gets louder the image should grow in size and not become congested, the bass should not overwhelm the other instruments, and the size of the room should remain constant and discernible.

It might seem a bit overwhelming at first, but if you repeat this track enough times you'll come to know and trust it as I do. Once it's familiar, any little changes in tonality, clarity, image size, depth, height, or width will become obvious to you. You are now intimate with the music. You can, as we like to say, see into the recording.

GOING BIG

We've also included a couple of acoustic firework tracks on the Audiophile's Guide setup recording, so that you may see how effortlessly your system handles a track with extreme dynamics and full frequency extension. These are fun tracks that should be enjoyed after you feel you've done the work of setup and are ready to take off the training wheels.

As I mentioned in the beginning of this chapter, it's a bit overwhelming to start with a big piece—like the ones you'll find on Tracks 17, 18, and 19—because there's so much going on. To really enjoy them you're going to need to turn off the audio microscope, turn down the lights, crank up the volume, and just let 'er rip. Let the music wash over you as you drift away. These tracks are the finishing touches, the end pieces you can use to show off the system or simply put a smile on your face.

DIVERSITY IS THE KEY

Once you learn what to listen for in recordings it's now time to put together a library of favorites. In my tuning collection, for example, I have well over 100 selections featuring a wide range of diverse music and recordings. These are important because, while it's helpful to use only a few simple tracks while you're training your ear/brain to evaluate equipment and setup choices, you don't want to adjust your system to only fit a small handful of recording types. Instead, aim for a system that treats all recordings and musical genres with respect and truthful reproduction.

Pay attention to the space between the performers. This is where we can expect realism

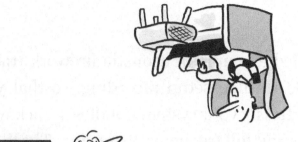

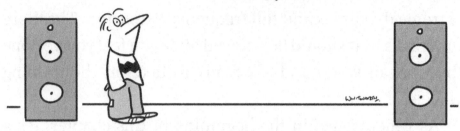

On a great system
even poorly recorded
music does not upset
the listener's
experience

"I'VE FOUND THE PERFECT PLACEMENT FOR MY LISTENING SEAT."

Here's the process I use when evaluating a new piece of equipment like a cable, speaker, or another part of the electronic chain. First, I use my familiar simple-to-medium tracks to make quick comparisons between the new and the old setups. Should I be pleased at the improvements I hear with the new component, I then spend time making sure those changes aren't specific to the small sampling of music. To do that, I go through a dozen or so diverse tracks to see if there's any common trait. For example, if I were evaluating a new power cable and upon first listen to my simple tracks I found it to be a step forward in musical truth—perhaps offering a much cleaner, clearer view into the music—my next step would be to run through multiple styles and genres to make sure nothing had been lost or inappropriately added. I play everything from folk to jazz to orchestral selections. To assure myself that there were no subtle details lost, I make sure to zero in on instruments with lots of upper harmonics and nuanced overtones. Some tracks in my hundred or more references have pants-rattling bass notes; are they still there? Other tracks are particularly focused on delicate treble regions: brushed cymbals, musical shakers, boomwhackers, cabasas, and castanets. How are they presented—natural and lifelike as before? Or exaggerated and strident, as sometimes happens when we find a cable or equipment that seems clearer?

If, in the end, everything sounds like itself, without too much interference from this or that, then I can be reasonably confident in the audible improvements.

WHAT KINDS OF MUSIC WORK BEST AND WHY

Not all recordings and musical types sound great. In fact, there's more poorly recorded music out there than you can shake a stick at. That's why experienced audiophiles create playlists filled with the best recordings. As previously mentioned, I have more than a hundred tracks I keep on hand for equipment evaluation, stored as a playlist on my favorite streaming service, Qobuz. If you have Qobuz, you can go to https://open.qobuz.com/playlist/2198171 and enjoy PS Audio's reference playlist.

The majority of these tracks were chosen with several criteria in mind. First and foremost, they are all excellent representations of the recording art for their genre. You can count on them to offer proper soundstage and tonal balance within the space they were intended. Second, they are musically interesting, enjoyable, and diverse enough to warrant their use as a reference library. It's important for audiophiles to have a proper reference set of discs or tracks at the ready. Without access to known quality

Of course you have your arsenal of great tracks, but don't rely solely on them for evaluation

recordings, there is no way to reliably evaluate the system's performance or to make valid judgments of equipment and setup choices.

One of the worst things you can do is take a recording that sounded good on a pair of earbuds, the car radio, or a friend's casual system and rely on it for a reference track. That would be like studying for a PhD by only reading half-baked Twitter posts! Instead, use and develop known references that you can consistently reply upon. Once you've worked your way through the reference material, then it's perfectly acceptable—even encouraged—to play anything and everything you wish, from poorly recorded head-banging grunge to old monophonic classics. Because you've relied for setup on approved reference materials, you're now able to judge the quality of recordings for what they are, as opposed to guessing.

Room Tuning Techniques

The Point of First Reflection

If you want to get a bit more specific in your use of furniture (or other methods) to tame the room's acoustics, you can focus your efforts on what is known as the Point of First Reflection.

Even if you're not going to make much ado about this step, it's always helpful to know where the point of first reflection is

Direct sound from the loudspeakers arrives at the listener's ears before the reflected sound does. First reflections are signals that have bounced off the walls, ceiling, and floors to arrive at the listening position later in time, mixing with the direct signal. They are called early or first reflections when they are received within 20 milliseconds (20 thousandths of a second) of the direct sound. When these occur, they are too quick for the brain to sort them out as delayed copies, so they are perceived as part of the original direct sound. This alters the music's tonal balance and wreaks havoc on imaging. As you may know, there are two ways to deal with them: absorb or diffuse. But first, you need to find the point along the wall they will first reflect off of.

To identify the point of first reflection, you will need the help of an accomplice who isn't overly concerned with looking a little goofy while holding a small mirror. First, remove the grilles on your loudspeakers. While you're seated in your listening position, have your assistant stand with his/her back touching the sidewall. They should position themselves halfway between the right speaker and your seating position, holding the mirror directly in front of them and parallel to the sidewall behind them.

Your job is to look at the image in the mirror and ask

your assistant to move toward or away from the speaker until you can see the right speaker's tweeter in the center of the mirror. Mark this spot with a bit of tape on the floor. This is the point of first reflection, where the sound from the right tweeter and midrange first strikes the wall and then reflects off. Using a tape measure, mark the same spot on the opposite wall for the left channel.

Depending on how lively your room is, or your personal preferences, you can now absorb or diffuse the wall at the point of first reflection. I am generally a proponent of diffusion as opposed to absorption. The problem with absorption is that it's nearly impossible to evenly absorb all frequencies. Diffusion, on the other hand, evenly scatters the sound so that when the delayed signal hits your ear, it is diffuse rather than specific, which makes it easier for the brain to ignore.

Now that you know where the point of first reflection is, you can choose what to do with that information. The simplest way to diffuse or absorb the sound is to place a physical object on or near the wall. This could be as simple as placing a tall plant or as involved as moving in a tall and narrow bookshelf.

DIFFUSERS VS. ABSORBERS

As previously mentioned, there are two ways of taming a room with acoustic treatments: diffusion or absorption. In general, diffusion works best as frequencies rise while absorption is better used when handling bass.

DIFFUSION

A diffuser removes the specificity of an image or a sound. In optics, we might use a slightly frosted glass or even

It's best to have a wide variety of music including acoustic, synth, classical, pop, and whatever floats your boat

put a piece of muslin (cheesecloth) over the camera lens, to soften the image by scattering the light. In acoustics, we can break up and scatter soundwaves with furniture, plants, book-laden shelving, or commercially available specialized panels called diffusers.

Diffusers work best at frequencies above several hundred hertz: at the middle to top of the range of the human voice. Diffusers work by scattering the sound field in many directions. There are multiple types of diffusers: Maximum Length Sequence, Quadratic-residue, Primitive-root, Optimized, and Two-dimensional hemispherical, among others with fancy-sounding names. What they all have in common is an uneven surface off which the sound can reflect at differing angles and/or distances. These can range from manufactured versions, some of which look like a jumble of staggered children's blocks on the wall, to elegant strips of varying-depth wooden slats. Perhaps the most natural of diffusers is a bookshelf filled with books of differing depth. In one of my music rooms I built floor-to-ceiling bookshelves into the wall at the points of first reflection, as well as on the wall behind my loudspeakers. I then canvassed the local thrift stores to purchase hundreds of cheap books of all sizes to fill those shelves. It looked great and sounded great too.

Because universally absorbing all frequencies in the range of human hearing borders on impossible, it's often best to turn to diffusion for frequencies above 200Hz. Furthermore, too much absorption at any frequency can acoustically deaden a room to the point of sounding lifeless. The best rooms are those with a judicious blend

Diffusers are my favorite tools to bring a sense of open spacious sound to the room

of both absorption and diffusion. Diffusers maintain the room's "live" ambience, increase spaciousness, and at the same time reduce standing waves and slap echo.

ABSORPTION

If a room is too lively and echo-sounding, or too bass-heavy, it may be necessary to eliminate some of that unwanted acoustic energy instead of scattering it. You can reduce the actual volume of sound at specific frequencies by absorbing them.

As mentioned earlier, absorbers work by converting sound into heat by means of friction. Sound is generated from organized pressure waves while heat is characterized by chaotic movement. If you can channel the organized pressure waves into an acoustical labyrinth that disorganizes its energy and generates friction with the many porous pathways, you can dissipate some of the sound in the form of heat. Try talking through a scarf and you'll scatter enough focused energy over rough porous surfaces to generate the heat that muffles your voice. With a light fabric, only higher frequencies are absorbed through the process of friction, but thicker ones (or multiple layers) can affect almost all the frequencies.

Cloth chairs, sofas, and thick rugs and drapes do a good job of absorbing most frequencies, but they are particularly effective at upper frequencies. Put too many plush pillows and furniture in a heavily draped and carpeted room and you might start to suck some of the life out.

Generally you'll want to work more with diffusers than absorbers

A moderate amount of soft, sound-absorbing furniture in a room typically provides enough absorption, so adding more is usually only needed to help mitigate problems with our old nemesis, bass. As I noted in the basic speaker

"QUICK - RUN! IT'S A BASS TRAP!"

and listening position setup chapters, bass waves build up in the room, requiring the perfect listening spot that isn't overwhelmed (or underwhelmed) with low-frequency energy. Bass buildup is particularly intense in the corners of the room, and it is here that you can add what is known as a bass trap.

There are numerous commercially available bass traps

THE BASS TRAP

There are two main types of absorptive bass traps: resonant and porous. Both are effective, but one—the porous absorber—is a more practical alternative for home stereo systems. A resonant absorber is difficult to design and implement because it needs to be mechanically tuned to resonate in sympathy with the specific frequencies being absorbed. This process requires careful measurement analysis, combined with a deep knowledge of acoustics and mathematics. A porous absorber, on the other hand, does not resonate and thus it need not be tuned or measured. We could say the porous absorber is the more plug-and-play choice for a bass trap.

Porous absorbers are typically made from mineral wool, fiberglass, or foam, all substances that resist the passage of air molecules and, through friction, convert bass frequencies into heat. This type of bass trap is often found in the form of tall and round tubes or rectangular panels, surrounded by multiple connected layers of the absorbing materials and faced with paper or foil. This facing improves low bass absorption by translating the compression of air on the foil or paper surface into physical compression of the fibers that are in contact with it.

These round or rectangular bass traps are most effective at reducing unwanted bass energy when placed in the room's corners, but they also can help along the room's boundary walls. Often, you'll see stacks of them in each of the room's four corners, forming a set of floor-to-ceiling columns.

Be careful not to over damp your room

PUTTING IT ALL TOGETHER

There's a lot to consider about the room and its interaction with your stereo speakers and listening position. Overall, you want natural sound. As I mentioned in an earlier chapter, I can walk into just about any room and tell if it's going to be alright for audio, simply by the sound of my movements, voice, and even just how my ears feel. As a quick aside, I remember the somewhat terrifying experience of being locked in an anechoic chamber for the first time. An anechoic chamber is an acoustically dead room without any acoustic reflections at any frequency, and it's used to measure loudspeakers. As I heard the chamber's massive refrigerator-style door click shut, all outside sounds vanished. It was way too quiet and way too uncomfortable—my voice was swallowed whole, as if I were speaking into a vacuum cleaner's suction. After 15 minutes in the chamber, though, my ears had relaxed enough that I began noticing a strange rushing sound permeating the room. This was odd because no sound could enter this soundproof fortress. It wasn't until later that I learned the rushing noise was the sound of blood running through the veins of my ears—something always present but generally too quiet to notice.

In my reference system I have bass traps on the wall behind my listening position

With the goal of a natural-sounding environment in mind, you now have the tools to craft the best environment in which to play music. You can use rugs, drapes, and soft absorbing furniture to temper unwanted liveliness and hard reflective surfaces to enliven the room. If you want a more spacious, better-defined sound, you can judiciously employ diffusers, often behind the loudspeakers on the front wall. These well-placed diffusers can add startling levels of depth and naturalness to the soundstage.

Great equipment in a bad room will rarely be as enjoyable as mediocre equipment in a great room. So here's the take-away: go easy on room tuning, be conscious of how the room sounds, and work with the room as a partner rather than an enemy. By following these rules, you can enhance your system's imaging and tonality, often making a bigger difference than the choice of equipment itself.

Panel Speaker Tuning

As mentioned in the section on speaker selection, panel speakers can be an excellent choice for those not bothered by their size or their eccentricities. Over the years, some of my favorite systems have featured panel speakers from Magnepan, Martin Logan, Sanders, Acoustat, Roger West, Infinity, and Quad. These tall and thin boxless speakers have both advantages and disadvantages. Here's a reminder.

Panel speakers are almost always dipoles

- The main advantages of a panel speaker are:
- Excellent high-frequency response
- Excellent transient response
- Amazing clarity
- Not big boxes

The main disadvantages of panel speakers are:
- Having to look at giant room dividers
- They often do not play loudly
- They can be tough for amplifiers to drive
- They have limited bass response
- They can be difficult to set up
- Very narrow listening area
- Their frames vibrate

For those who prefer panel speakers, I wanted to include some advice on setting up and tweaking them.

BASS AND DYNAMICS

The first consideration when working with panel speakers is their lack of both deep bass and dynamics. Panel speakers work by moving very small amounts of air in large areas of a thin membrane. Unlike a dynamic woofer's big pistonic movements of an inch or more, panel speakers are confined to mere fractions of inches. This means that to move enough air, the panels themselves must be quite large, typically larger than is practical in the average room. But even a large panel speaker will be limited in producing dynamic contrasts and low bass notes.

This failing of panel speakers—both in perceived dynamics and low frequency extension—can be solved by adding a subwoofer or subwoofer pair. All of my many reference-quality, panel-based speaker systems have been augmented by the addition of a "fast" subwoofer pair. Quite a few audiophiles may roll their eyes at that idea, as they generally believe that cone-driven subwoofers can never match the speed of thin-membraned panel speakers. Let me debunk that popular myth. While it is true that the significantly higher mass of cone drivers cannot move as quickly as the ultra-lightweight low-mass ribbon, electrostatic, and planar diaphragms, none of that matters if the frequency is low enough and the subwoofer's design is properly executed.

How Subwoofers Can Disappear

The trick to implementing a good subwoofer in any system is integrating it so you never actually hear the subwoofer as a separate entity. Instead, the goal is always to adjust the position and crossovers so that the main speakers sound as if they now have subterranean low frequencies.

Getting low bass out of panel speakers is problematic

This is easy to manage if you remember to keep the subwoofer's low pass filter (which determines how high the subwoofer plays) set low—somewhere between 30Hz and 50Hz, but ideally as close to 30Hz as possible. At these low frequencies, the "speed" of the subwoofer relative to that of the faster panel speaker doesn't matter as much because of the long wavelengths involved.

THE SUBWOOFER'S TRANSIENT "SPEED"

The idea of a fast or slow subwoofer is yet another misconception. Subwoofers cannot be fast because they do not produce high frequencies. They can, however, sound fast or slow because of something called step response, sometimes referred to as transient speed. When a high-mass object moves, there's resistance (inertia) to its changing states from standing still to moving in a direction. Inertia is what slams you against the seat belt when you hit the car's brakes and what pushes you back in the seat as you accelerate. It acts the same way given changes to the woofer cone's speed or direction of motion. A well-designed subwoofer has good control over the stopping and

"IF YOU ASK ME YOU CAN NEVER HAVE TOO MUCH WOOF."

starting of the woofer's motion, so it sounds fast, but in reality we're just not hearing any problems with its step response.

Blended properly, a well-setup sub disappears and suddenly the anemic panel speaker growls with authority and enjoys improved dynamics.

NARROW SWEET SPOTS

Depending on the type of panel speaker, the listening area is rather narrow compared to box speakers. Electrostatic panel speakers are generally thought to have the narrowest of sweet spots (the critical listening area) because of their extreme directionality at high frequencies, a function of the relatively large diaphragm surface area producing high frequencies. Ribbons and planars are less directional because they typically have smaller tweeter areas.

Regardless of which type of panel speaker you are working with, you are going to have the biggest listening sweet spot if, in the grid setup procedure, you do your best to use as little toe in as possible. Here you'll be better served by scooting the left and right channels closer together to solidify the center image. On PS Audio's all-ribbon panel speaker reference system, the Infinity IRSV, we have a reasonably wide sweet spot, which we achieved by moving the left and right channels close together and limiting toe in to a few degrees.

Bracing the panels speaker's frames can offer a big benefit in image specificity

TITLING THE PANELS

As mentioned, most panel speakers are more directional than most box speakers, because of the relatively large

"IT'S GOT TO BE BOX – I'M
NOT HAVING ANYTHING
IN THE HOUSE THAT'S
THINNER THAN ME."

*To test, use a CD
or two placed
under the front
or the back of the
panel speaker's
base*

surface areas used to generate higher frequencies. With a smaller tweeter or midrange, the total acoustic energy is generated from a smaller surface area and, in partnership with the front baffle, it's easier to aim all that acoustic energy at the listener's ears. A large panel speaker outputs the same level of acoustic energy, but because that energy is spread out over a much larger area it becomes far more difficult to deliver all that sound pressure to your ears. I like to imagine the problem like pouring water into a bottle. The small tweeter is like a funnel—it's easy to pour water into the bottle. But the large plane of the panel speaker makes it more like a Mason jar trying to fill the bottle without benefit of a funnel, so transferring water to the bottle takes more effort—without care, most of the water would never make it through the bottle's narrow neck.

Once you have your best setup for center image fill, as wide a sweet spot as possible, and as much depth as is practical, you may find the high frequencies to be lacking (or sometimes the opposite). One easy fix for this is to tilt the panels forward for more treble energy or backwards for less. This technique, in effect, aims the higher frequencies at or away from the listener and it can be quite effective.

The panel speaker's driver technologies of ribbons and planars are available in box speakers as well

"There is two kinds of music, the good, and the bad. I play the good kind."

Louis Armstrong

Advanced Equipment Choices

The Importance of Cables

I n order to build an audio system based on separate components, we have to rely on connecting cables. Using high-quality interconnect, speaker, and power cables is of vital importance to maximizing your system's audio performance.

There are few subjects more controversial than cables and the role they play

The idea that cables make an audible difference raises many proverbial neck-hairs, especially among dyed-in-the-wool engineering types. In my years of running a high-end audio company, few components have prompted more debate than cables—especially power cables. Google has helpfully immortalized quite a few pundits lambasting and ridiculing me for my views on cables. They've called me everything from snake oil salesman to charlatan, not to mention a few expletives that I probably shouldn't repeat here.

But here's the truth: every audiophile knows that cables matter. This isn't just voodoo or pseudo-science, as the audio world's skeptics and self-proclaimed experts would like us to believe. To anyone who has taken the time to make an actual side-by-side comparison of cable types on a high-resolution audio system, the differences are not only real but significant enough to pay close attention to. For if you're hoping to breathe magic into your sound system, you're going to have to pay attention to everything in the audio chain that matters. And cables matter. A lot.

Fortunately, the price-to-performance ratio we often see with audio electronics and speakers isn't as applicable to cables. Certainly, there are outrageously expensive,

"OF COURSE IT SOUNDS FULL —
IT'S JUST SWALLOWED
A ROOM."

often overpriced, cables (the ones in Music Room Two at PS Audio exceed $100,000 at retail), but for the most part, careful listening and matching can make a major improvement without a great deal of expense. On my own system, several very low-cost USB and HDMI cables outperformed more expensive ones. It just took a bit of experimenting and trial and error to find them.

THE FIRST RULE OF CABLES

Cables do not enhance sound—they only make it worse. My friend Bill Low, of Audioquest, is fond of saying the task of the cable is to do no harm, and he's right. The best you can hope for with interconnecting cables is to do as little damage as possible. You don't want the treble rolled

Cables cannot enhance, only detract. Rely upon synergy between cable and equipment shortcomings to more closely match your musical tastes

off or the bass squeezed out of the music. With cables, nothing is perfect—there's no magic cable construction that will get you everything you want. Every model of interconnect, speaker, or power cable will at least subtly (and sometimes not so subtly) impact how your system sounds.

As with other audio equipment, a company's reputation can help you locate good cables, but mostly it's a matter of matching them to your components by ear. But some generalizations are still helpful, in terms of how certain types of cable and their construction impact sound quality. For example, cable conductors of copper are said to sound softer and fuller in the lower-end frequencies than those constructed of silver, which is thought to be thinner and brighter sounding. Unfortunately, while there may be some truth to these observations, they are neither universal nor inviolate. Thus, I cannot say with any certainty that if you do this you will hear that. I truly wish it were easier, but there's a good reason audiophile forums feature thousands of posts bickering back and forth about what works best with what. That is because when cables are mated to equipment, there is either a synergistic or a dysergistic result based on the entire audio chain, room, musical choice, and personal tastes of the listener—which means there's no standard on which to rely.

AUDIO SYNERGY

The dictionary describes synergy as the interaction or co-operation of two or more agents to produce a combined effect greater than the sum of their separate effects (dysergy has the opposite effect). In terms of cables, that means getting their small imperfections to play nicely with

Synergy comes from balancing the strengths and weaknesses of equipment

the strengths and shortcomings of your electronics and speakers. You've already learned in earlier chapters that there's no such thing as perfect speakers or electronics. So like a master chef, try to bring out the audio flavors you want and subdue those that will detract from the track's overall taste.

I think of the audio system's cabling like a chain. Each link depends on its connection for the strength of the whole. If your speakers sound thin in the midbass and you can't go any further in setup to correct for this weakness, your next best alternatives are to swap out components within the system or marry them with synergistic cables to ameliorate the problem.

"THAT'S THE MOST
RESPONSIVE
INTER-CONNECT
I'VE EVER HEARD."

There are no pat answers to choosing the right cables for your system. You will have to listen

Now, I'm not saying that you should use cables as equalizers, but the concept is similar—regardless of how repugnant it may seem to some audiophiles. When you're improving your system, you mainly want to use setup techniques and equipment choices to correct shortcomings and enhance strengths. But once you've exhausted those options, it's perfectly fine to turn to the cables to finish the job. Just remember: don't rely upon cables as a crutch, but rather treat them as the finishing touch.

FINDING THE RIGHT CABLES

I wish I could wave a magic wand and give you a list of the best cables to fit the job at hand, but I can't. Cables are an ongoing challenge, even for me: I outfit my system as best I can, and then along comes some new cable that changes everything—and I just have to try it. It can be a bit maddening at times.

You will be told more than once that cable differences are all in your head. Audion for yourself and make your own mind up

Here's my advice, for whatever it's worth: when it comes to cables, concentrate on musical truth more than flashy sound effects. Audiophile sound effects are like brass rings: they shine as brightly as gold and beckon us to grab them, but they turn out to be more sparkling glint than valuable substance. A cable that enriches highs often does so at the expense of a solid bass response; that exaggerated depth may be appealing, but only until we notice that it's at the expense of tonal balance.

Take your time and remember that with cables, you get what you pay attention to through listening. Audition, audition, audition. Your job is to do as little harm as possible while attaining the greatest level of synergy between your equipment. Keeping all the bits and bobs in the audio chain as close as possible to music's truth means that sometimes, you have to forego the spectacular to get a good dose of the accurate. In the end, you'll be happier when you do.

The Importance of AC Power

AC power and its importance in the high-end audio chain is perhaps even more controversial than even cables

Here's a subject near and dear to my heart: AC power. Everything you hear on your audio system began as an AC sine wave coming out of your home's wall. In the US, that sinewave is at 120 volts and smoothly moves between plus and minus 60 times per second. In Europe, Russia, Africa, the Mideast, and much of Asia and Australia, the sinewave is twice the US level at 230 volts, and it gently moves between plus and minus a bit slower, at 50 times per second. Just like the purity of water determines how it's going to taste, the quality of that AC has a lot to do with how your system is going to sound.

Simply plugging your stereo directly into the wall socket will never be as good as what you can accomplish with modern AC power technology. Like cables, this too is a major source of controversy. Self-proclaimed pundits and fully qualified engineers alike just love to make fun of me and the audiophile community for our stance on the importance of AC power, and what good sport it must be too. It's easy to make fun of something when you've never really investigated what difference it makes to serious users. If you're in need of a little heartburn, excitement, or both, head over to the audio forums on PSAudio.com and read the bitter debates between those who hear the differences and those who cannot bring themselves to even give them the time of day.

My goal here is not to prove the importance of AC power to a system's sound reproduction. I, like many advanced

"I ASKED YOU TO MAKE THE SPEAKERS DISAPPEAR NOT TURN THEM INTO RABBITS."

audiophiles, already know the importance of AC power. But I do want to explain what's important to get right and how best to go about it. And as you know by now, I rarely shy away from the chance to tell a story to help with understanding.

A few years ago, Richard Murrison—a fellow engineer and contributor to our free online magazine, Copper—asked to borrow a set of our electronics to demonstrate at the 2015 Montreal High-End show. We sent him our best: a pair of BHK 300 monoblock amplifiers and a P15 Power Plant AC regenerator to power them. Richard was using the amps for his room's demo system, which consisted of a pair of Wilson Audio Sasha loudspeakers. After the show, Richard phoned me to express his utter joy at how good the system sounded and to ask if he could purchase the BHK amplifiers. (He returned the Power Plant AC regenerator a couple days later, with his thanks.) A month later, he called me quite embarrassed because he wanted to return the amps. Seems the BHK 300s powering the very same pair of Wilson Sashas didn't even sound close to what he had heard in the small hotel room at the tradeshow.

AC power is the foundation of everything we listen to in our music systems

Richard was flummoxed because everything was the same as he had set it up at the show: same amps, same speakers, same source, same cables, same music... everything except for one piece of gear. At my urging, he allowed me to ship him back the P15 Power Plant, just to see what would happen. One week later, I got another call from a decidedly sheepish Richard. As an engineer, he had assumed the Power Plant was little more than a fancy power conditioner and, as such, it wasn't all that important. He now understood his mistake. The addition of the power regenerator, which provided fully rebuilt and regulated AC power to those two amplifiers, had made all the difference in the world. Try as he might, he couldn't go back to the old system: the magic just wasn't the same.

Cleaning the AC line of noise is not the most important consideration when it comes to AC power

AC POWER: PROTECTION

There are three main areas of concern when it comes to AC power: protection, noise reduction, and regulation and purity. The first and third are considerably more important.

For the most part, AC power is quite safe in the first world, though not infallible. After a power outage, whether from downed utility poles after a storm or the occasional exploding power transformer, there can be a potentially damaging surge of voltage when power returns. Should there be a lightning storm or other anomaly on the line, voltage spikes and power surges can also enter the home and damage your sensitive audio electronics.

A simple surge protector is usually enough to save your gear from damage. These devices work using a voltage clamping device known as an MOV, and for the most part they are very effective. However, they have a downside for audiophiles: since the surge suppressor is usually in an extension strip at the end of a skinny unshielded power cord, the cheap construction can have negative sonic impacts for your system. Your best bet is to go with a high-end audio company's power product that has AC protection built right in. But if that's not an option for you, then you're better off using a power suppressor that plugs directly into the AC socket without a cord.

AC POWER: NOISE REDUCTION

If you read the Hi-Fi magazines and visit the audio forums, you're likely to see a lot of controversy over AC power conditioners and isolation transformers. These devices are either inline power filters or magnetically coupled power transformers, designed to remove and isolate high-frequency noises generated by cellphones, radio stations, and other radio frequency (RF) interference. For the most part, they do an admirable job at lowering noise before the AC power gets into your audio equipment. That's the good news. The problem with AC power conditioners and isolation transformers is twofold: 1) RF and other airborne noises on the line don't have a major impact on sound quality, and 2) eliminating them comes at a cost.

Most well-designed high-end audio products effectively lower incoming RF right at the point where the AC enters the chassis. What remains is typically eliminated by the power supply itself before it's converted into the audio you hear. And there's another problem. AC power conditioners work by inserting in-line power filters that raise the impedance of the AC line—a problem with isolation transformers as well, though for different reasons. When

AC protection doesn't have to come with a sonic price

this happens, you often lose precious musical information such as fine inner detail, upper harmonics like the ringing of a plucked string, and you often get sloppier bass.

This is not to suggest that power conditioners and isolation transformers have no positive impacts on sound quality. Systems that are powered through them often sound cleaner with a quieter noise floor, but at the expense of getting a slightly bleached sound devoid of life. The problem is choosing one: personally, I want a cleaner sound with a blacker background, while still preserving and enhancing inner details like string plucks and cymbal shimmers.

AC POWER: REGULATION AND PURITY

The holy grail for AC power would be to have a big, coal-burning, black-smoke-belching power plant, humming away in your backyard. Unfortunately, your property value might suffer a bit. Instead, most of us use centralized power stations that feed an entire city. We share our AC power with industry, our neighbors, and even the grumpy old guy down the street. The more power is shared, the worse its quality. That quality affects the available voltage in the AC sinewave's peak, which is used to top up your equipment's power supply capacitors. Worse, given the hundreds of feet of copper wire between the utility pole and your AC socket, the problem with impedance mentioned earlier gets worse. There are a few ways to effectively remedy these problems, so let's start with the simplest and least expensive first.

Dedicated lines are often the least expensive improvements you can make to your high-performance system

Dedicated Lines

One way to minimize the problems with AC power is by wiring in a system known as the dedicated line. In most homes, a single power cable is strung through the wall, feeding multiple outlets. You've no doubt seen that when a circuit breaker pops, multiple appliances or lights lose power. A dedicated line can make for as little sharing of power as possible.

If you have the luxury of new construction or you hire a good electrician, you can specify a dedicated circuit breaker, wire, and AC outlet for each piece of equipment in your chain. By running individual circuits and in-wall power cabling to equipment, you will minimize the interaction between amps, preamps, and DACs, as well as lower the impedance if you go with heavier gauge wire (my preference is 10-gauge).

If you can manage it, have your electrician install a separate 20-amp circuit breaker (for setups in the US) and 12- or even 10-gauge wire feeding each AC receptacle in the system. Dedicating these power lines so each piece has its own AC power cable, going back to one common point in your home, can yield major sonic benefits without spending a lot of money.

AC Regeneration

An AC regenerator can complement or even replace a dedicated line, and it isn't affected by the quality of the incoming AC. Homes with highly distorted or shared power lines, which are common in apartment buildings and condo complexes (or just from sharing a power grid with your neighbors) can still have perfect power, unaffected by sharing, downstream issues, or the length of wire connecting them to the utility pole.

Low impedance, regulated AC power is the key to great sound

AC regenerators work in the same way a boiled water distillation system does. Instead of filtering out impurities, a water distillation system first boils dirty water into steam, leaving all impurities behind, then distills the steam back to water. An AC regenerator, similarly, takes the incoming AC sinewave, converts it to pure DC (like a battery voltage), leaving behind any AC problems with purity or impedance shortfalls, then regenerates new and perfect, low-impedance AC to feed your equipment.

AC regenerators are not cheap. They are, in fact, big power amplifiers that are costly to build, but they're remarkably effective at powering equipment. In fact, AC regeneration has been used for years in laboratories and medical applications where pure, perfect power is required. Their results are impressive. Regardless of the incoming AC fluctuations or the length of impedance producing wire between the utility pole and your home, the regenerator outputs low-distortion, pure, tightly regulated, and low-impedance AC power. The results are immediately apparent to even casual listeners.

Whatever you choose to do with AC power in your system, I would encourage you not to ignore its importance. All the fancy equipment in the world is better served when the source of its energy is strong, pure, and unaffected by its neighbors. Just like a gourmet meal requires high-quality ingredients, a great stereo system requires high-quality AC power.

Do Measurements Matter?

There is perhaps no greater debate in high-end audio than that between the Subjectivists and Objectivists—those who believe the ear is the ultimate measuring tool vs. those who believe our test equipment reigns superior. In my view, both parties are right and the dogmatists on both sides are missing the point. Objective measurements and subjective experience are complementary elements of the whole Hi-Fi experience. Measurements give us a clue but listening is what matters.

Trust manufacturers that place as much emphasis on listening as they do measuring

Many audio manufacturers assume that if a piece of equipment measures great, then it must also sound great. Others are stumped when a unit that sounds great doesn't have equally great measurements. They chalk the mismatch between measurements and sound quality up to the unknown. It turns out, though, that this simplistic, mechanistic view of human conscious experience is flat-out wrong.

The human experience—especially when it comes to sound—is not something that can be measured. Brain science is nowhere near the point where we can use equipment to assess or measure consciousness, specifically what makes for a pleasurable and rewarding listening experience. While we have technology that can measure the different objective elements of sound created by one piece of equipment, human perception emerges as something greater than just the sum of its measurable parts.

We're comfortable suggesting that sound is subjective when it comes to our differences in perception, but often get uncomfortable when we speak of it in absolute terms. In other words, we believe the source of sound to be absolute but the perception of sound to be a matter of personal choice, one related to consciousness, agency, personhood, reality, and truth—and based on or influenced by personal feelings, tastes, and opinions.

Measurement gives a valuable read on performance, but it does not necessarily align directly with the listener's experience. Moreover, in real life people are not hearing the same things, even when they are sitting in the same room at the same time, listening to the same music from the same stereo system. What one particular listener may consider superior is driven by her personal preferences, which will differ from those of another listener. The ultimate value of stereo equipment has to be measured by each listener's personal experience: many people enjoy listening to gear that does not measure well, while others report poor listening experiences coming from equipment that measures great. Listening for enjoyment is subjective and imperfect.

I was recently reminded of this puzzle when PS Audio senior design engineer Darren Myers was working on the Stellar Phono Stage. He had that beauty measuring a perfect ten, yet he was unhappy with the sound. It certainly wasn't dreadful, but it was closed and restricted when the THD and IM were at their lowest. As he lifted the feedback levels that offered such great measurements, the sound opened up and blossomed. It was truly a thing of beauty to witness. This is just one more reason why Hi-Fi products must be designed with one foot in

Remember that what we hear is a combination of our ears and our brains. Our emotional state matters

"SUPERB PHANTOM CHANNEL."

the measurement lab and the other firmly planted in the listening room.

So, if the source of sound is absolute but hearing it is subjective, what's an equipment manufacturer to do? Cater to the subjective or the absolute? This interesting question has always been a source of both inspiration and balance for me and my colleagues at PS Audio. On one hand, the challenge of recreating the absolute sound has driven our design efforts for years. On the other hand, building equipment that pleases our subjective side has also guided our products since the day we started. After all, if it doesn't sound right when we're playing music, who cares if it measures great?

When it comes to the listening experience, the rubber meets the road when we use our ears as the final

The subjective vs. objective debates on this subject will likely rage on well past our lifetimes

measurement tool. Each of us has different ways of measuring what is good or bad, and at the end of the day, what measures well doesn't always sound good or appeal to each and every listener. Products have to be evaluated in terms of their ultimate use and performance, so any company that pushes measurements over listening is one to be questioned.

If it doesn't sound like music then how it measures doesn't much matter to listeners

Still, measurements of audio equipment, using sophisticated test gear, form an important part of the story and provide a steady reference. They're also a good way to judge the expertise and capabilities of a designer. At PS Audio we rely intensively on measurements when designing and building our equipment in the lab, but that is only the first step in the design process. The next takes place in the listening room, where the art is to combine the finest measurement equipment in the world with the best sets of ears. Between the two, we are able to offer products that makes music sound like, well, music.

Good audio equipment is designed to honor the absolute without sacrificing musicality. It is that balance between the absolute and the subjective that forms greatness. You cannot know how a piece of audio gear will sound in your system or home from mere measurements. You must use your own ears or the ears of others you trust. Like a chef following a recipe, it only works if you taste the dish.

Appendix

PS Audio Reference Music Tracks

Don't Know Why - Norah Jones - Come Away with Me
Dark Angel - Blue Rodeo - Five Days in July
Angel Vengador - Harry Gregson-Williams - Man on Fire
A case of you - Diana Krall - Live in Paris
Everything Is Free (feat. Flock of Dimes) - Sylvan Esso - Don't Dream
It's Over / Everything Is Free
Come Away with Me - Norah Jones - Come Away with Me
Gaia - James Taylor - Hourglass
On a Black Horse / Linearity - Avishai Cohen (b) - Almah
Get Lucky - Daft Punk feat. Pharrell Williams - Random Access Memories
(Hi-Res Version)
Goodbye Blue Sky - Pink Floyd - The Wall
Landslide - Fleetwood Mac - Fleetwood Mac (Deluxe Edition)
How Insensitive - Diana Krall - From This Moment On
Liquid Spirit - Gregory Porter - The Best of Blue Note
Gnomus - Jean Victor Arthur Guillou - Mussorgsky: M.P.: Pictures at an
Exhibition - Stravinski: 3 Movements from Petrushka
Quarter Chicken Dark - Yo-Yo Ma - Yo-Yo Ma - The Classic Albums
Collection
Raven - GoGo Penguin - A Humdrum Star
California Dreamin' - Diana Krall - Wallflower (Deluxe Edition)
San Jacinto - Peter Gabriel - Peter Gabriel 4: Security (Remastered)
Scarlet Town - Brad Mehldau - Chris Thile & Brad Mehldau
Seven Years - Norah Jones - Come Away with Me
Sleeping by Myself - Julian Lage & Chris Eldridge - Mount Royal
Stimela (The Coal Train) - Hugh Masekela - Hope
Finale: Presto - Ludwig van Beethoven - Debut

Take This Hammer (feat. The Fairfield Four) - Willie Watson - Folksinger, Vol. 2

Tennis Court - Lorde - Pure Heroine

The Ragpicker's Dream - Mark Knopfler - The Ragpicker's Dream

The Song Is You - Joe Pass - Virtuoso

The Tennessee Waltz - Allan Taylor - Behind the Mix

The Time Machine - Jean Michel Jarre - Electronica 1: The Time Machine

Train Song - Holly Cole - Temptation

Turn Me On - Norah Jones - Come Away with Me

Variations on One String on a Theme By Rossini: Moses Fantasie - Janos Starker - Janos Starker: Virtuoso Music for Cello

Warm Ways - Fleetwood Mac - Fleetwood Mac (Deluxe Edition)

Welcome to the Machine - Pink Floyd - Wish You Were Here

Within - Daft Punk - Random Access Memories (Hi-Res Version)

Youth - Daughter - A Long Way Down - Original Motion Picture Soundtrack

Mozart: Sonate in D-Dur Für Zwei Klaviere Kv 448: Allegro Con Spirito - Dena Piano Duo - The Nordic Sound

Nordheim: Colorazione - Cikada Duo - Nordheim

Islandsmoen: Requiem - Lacrymosa - Kristiansand Symfoniorkester - The Nordic Sound

Gjeilo: North Country II - Tom Barber - The Nordic Sound

Stairway to Heaven - Rodrigo y Gabriela - Rodrigo y Gabriela (Reedition Digitale)

Diving Duck Blues - Taj Mahal & Keb' Mo' - TajMo

Hip-Notica - Tony Hymas - Who Else!

Keep the Wolves Away - Uncle Lucius - And You Are Me

1br/1ba - Vienna Teng - Dreaming Through the Noise

Musical Genocide - Gregory Porter - Liquid Spirit

Arms of A Woman - Amos Lee - Amos Lee

Gomni (with Ry Cooder) - Ali Farka TourÈ - Talking Timbuktu (with Ry Cooder)

Trouble's What You're In - Fink - Wheels Turn Beneath My Feet

Line 'em Up - James Taylor - Hourglass

Run Away - Sarah Jarosz - Follow Me Down

Alison - Holly Cole - The Best of Holly Cole

Gaslighting Abbie - Steely Dan - Two Against Nature (Edition Studio Masters)

Where Will I Be - Emmylou Harris - Wrecking Ball

Sex in a Pan - Bela Fleck - UFO Tofu

Requiem: Pie Jesu - Mass Text - Rutter: Requiem - Five Anthems

Fanfare for the Common Man - Aaron Copland - Copland: Fanfare for the Common Man - Appalachian Spring - Symphony No. 3

Raleigh and Spencer - Tony Furtado - Tony Furtado Band

Harlem Nocturne - Illinois Jacquet - Swing's the Thing

Celestial Echo - Malia - Convergence

Samurai Cowboy - Various Interprets - The Gate

Swallow Your Pride - Rhys - Swallow Your Pride

Mose Allison Played Here - Greg Brown - Slant 6 Mind

Alexandra Leaving - Leonard Cohen - The Essential Leonard Cohen

Cowgirl in The Sand - Neil Young - Live at Massey Hall 1971

My Romance - Gene Ammons - Boss Tenor

Fever - Petra Magoni - Musica Nuda - Live FIP

Lost and Lookin' - Sam Cooke - The Man Who Invented Soul

Yesterday - Boyz II Men - II

Be Brave - My Brightest Diamond - All Things Will Unwind

Life on Mars? - Seu Jorge - The Life Aquatic with Steve Zissou

Hey Now - London Grammar - If You Wait (Deluxe)

Asheville Skies - The Milk Carton Kids - Monterey

Love Is A Verb - John Mayer - Born and Raised

Once You - Jacob Collier - Djesse Vol.1

Don't Mess with Mister T - Jeff Goldblum & The Mildred Snitzer Orchestra - The Capitol Studios Sessions

Don't Even Sing About It - The Books - The Lemon of Pink (Remastered)

Like I Was Sayin' - Chick Corea - Chinese Butterfly

Thanks to You - Boz Scaggs - Dig

Whiskey and You - Chris Stapleton - Traveler

Brother Can You Spare a Dime - George Michael - Songs from the Last Century

Take Five - Dave Brubeck - Time Out

Skin - Jamie Woon - Making Time

Friend of the Devil - Bob Weir - Dear Jerry: Celebrating the Music of Jerry Garcia

*Dance with Wave*s - Anouar Brahem - The Astounding Eyes of Rita

Pärt: Credo for Piano Solo, Mixed Choir and Orchestra - Arvo Pärt - Corigliano / Beethoven / Pärt "Credo"

So What - Miles Davis - Kind Of Blue

Nick of Time - Bonnie Raitt - Nick of Time

Opus One - Emmet Cohen - Masters Legacy Series Volume 2: Ron Carter

House Carpenter - Nickel Creek - This Side

(Improvvisazione) Adagio - Georg Friedrich Handel - Handel: Organ Concertos, Op.4

Sleeper - Snarky Puppy - We Like It Here

Voyeur - James Blake - Overgrown

Double Edge - Emika - Emika

Poco adagio - Olivier Latry - Francis Poulenc: Organ Concerto in G minor - Camille Saint-Saîns: Symphony No. 3, "Organ" - Samuel Barber: Toccata festiva

When the Party's Over - Billie Eilish - When We All Fall Asleep, Where Do We Go?

Bad Guy - Billie Eilish - When We All Fall Asleep, Where Do We Go?

You Don't Get Me High Anymore - Phantogram - Three

Deeper - Pete Belasco - Deeper

Fit Song - Cornelius - Sensuous

You Can't Fail Me Now - Bonnie Raitt - Slipstream

Infernal Dance of King Kaschei - Myung-Whun Chung - Rimsky-Korsakov: Scheherazade / Stravinsky: Firebird

Riverside - Agnes Obel - Philharmonics (Deluxe Edition)

No Tears Left to Cry - Ariana Grande - Sweetener (Explicit)

Kyrie - Jose Carreras - Ramirez: Missa Criolla; Navidad Nuestra; Navidad en Verano

Limehouse Blues - Bengt Hallberg - Jazz at the Pawnshop: 30th Anniversary

Someday House - Greg Brown - Freak Flag

Walking on Sacred Ground - Many Nations/ Thayne & Taiowa Hake - One Voice

With Every Breath I Take - Frank Sinatra - Close to You

111.   The Maze - Herbie Hancock - Jazz 'Til the End of the Night (All Tracks Remastered)

Jazz Variants - O-Zone Percussion Group - O-Zone Percussion Group: Bamba (La)

Glossary of Terms

Note: This glossary is designed to help you research and design your own two-channel home stereo system. For the definitions, I drew on several audio reference sources to complement my own lifetime of experience designing and building stereos.

A-weighting — A form of electrical filter which is designed to mirror the sensitivity of the human ear to different frequencies at low sound pressure levels. The filter rolls-off the low frequencies below about 700Hz and the highs above about 10kHz. This filter is often used when measuring low-level sounds, like the noise floor of a device.

Absolute phase, absolute polarity — The preservation of the initial acoustic waveform all the way through the recording and reproducing system, so that a compression that reaches the original microphone will be reproduced in the listener's system as a compression reaching his or her ears. A positive pressure on the microphone is reproduced as a positive pressure by the loudspeaker. For instance, the plosive "p" sound from a vocalist sends an initial positive air pressure wave toward the microphone, which responds with an initial inward movement of the microphone diaphragm, away from the vocalist, along with an identical positive air pressure wave at the loudspeaker.

AC — Alternating Current. In audio, signals are represented in the electrical domain as currents flowing alternately forward and back (+/-) in the circuits, an analog of the compression and rarefaction of acoustic air pressure. In electrical power, AC is an electric current which reverses direction 50 or 60 times per second depending on the region, in contrast to direct current (DC) which flows only in one direction, as in a battery.

Acoustic foam — A specific type of open-cell, expanded polyurethane that allows sound waves to enter and flow through the foam, absorbing their energy by means of conversion to heat through friction, and preventing them being reflected. The density and depth of the foam affects the frequency range over which it is effective as an absorber.

Acoustic treatment — A generic term embracing a range of products or constructions intended to absorb, diffuse, or reflect sound waves in a controlled manner, designed to improve the overall sound character of the room by reducing reflections through absorption and scattering acoustic energy through diffusion.

Acuity — The sensitivity of ears to very soft sounds through circumstance or training, used to hear and to assess the subtle qualitative attributes of reproduced sound.

Active circuit — Describes a circuit containing transistors, ICs, tubes, and other devices that require power to operate, and which are capable of amplification.

Active loudspeaker or monitor — A loudspeaker system in which the input signal is passed to a line-level crossover. Its suitably filtered outputs feed two (or more) power amplifiers, each connected directly to its own drive unit. The line-level crossover and amplifiers are usually (but not always) built into the loudspeaker cabinet.

A/D [A-D] converter — A device which converts an analog audio signal into a digital representation.

AES — Acronym for Audio Engineering Society, one of the industry's professional audio associations (www.aes.org).

Airy sound — The upper treble frequencies which sound light, delicate, open, and unrestricted in upper extension. A quality of reproduction systems that have very smooth and extended HF response.

Aliasing — When an analog signal is sampled for conversion into a digital data stream, the sampling frequency must be at least twice that of the highest frequency component of the input signal. Otherwise, the sampling process becomes inaccurate because there are insufficient points to define each cycle of the waveform, resulting in unwanted harmonic frequencies being added to the audible signal.

Ambience — The aurally perceived impression of an acoustical space, like the performing hall in which a recording was made.

Amp (Ampere) — Unit of electrical current (A).

Amp/amplifier — An electrical device that increases the voltage or power of an electrical signal. The amount of amplification can be specified as a multiplication factor (e.g. x10) or in decibels (e.g. 20dB).

Amplitude — The waveform signal level. It can refer to acoustic sound levels or electrical signal levels.

Analog — Analog circuitry uses a continually changing voltage or current to represent the audio signal. The electrical audio signal inside a piece of equipment can be thought of as 'analogous' to the original acoustic signal.

Attenuate — To reduce the signal amplitude or level.

Audio data compression — A system used to reduce the amount of data in an audio signal. Lossless audio data reduction systems (e.g. FLAC and ALAC) can fully and precisely reconstruct the original audio data with bit-accuracy, but the amount of data reduction is limited to 2:1. Lossy data audio reduction systems (e.g. MPEG, AAC, AC3, MP3, and others) permanently discard audio information that is deemed to have been 'masked' by more prominent sounds. The original data can never be retrieved, but the reduction in total data can be considerable (12:1 is common).

Audio frequency — Signals in the range of human audio audibility. Nominally 20Hz to 20kHz.

Balanced wiring — Two conductors, each carrying an audio signal of the opposite phase for the purpose of lowering common mode noise. Identical (balanced) impedances are used to ground from each of two signal-carrying conductors, which are enclosed within an all-embracing shield. This shield is grounded (to catch and remove unwanted RFI), but it plays no part in passing the audio signal or providing its voltage reference. Instead, the two signal wires provide the reference voltage for each other—each signal is conveyed 'differentially,' and the receiver detects the voltage difference between the two signal wires and rejects anything in common such as noise.

Band-pass filter (BPF) — A filter that removes or attenuates frequencies above and below the center frequency at which it is set, and which only passes a specific range of frequencies.

Bandwidth — The range of frequencies passed by an electronic circuit such as an amplifier. The frequency range is usually measured at the points where the level drops by 3dB relative to the maximum.

Bass response — The frequency response of a loudspeaker system at the lower end of the spectrum. The physical size and design of a loudspeaker cabinet and the bass driver (woofer) determine the system's low frequency extension (the lowest frequency the speaker can reproduce at normal level) and how quickly the signal level falls below that frequency.

Bit rate — The number of data bits replayed or transferred in a given period of time (normally one second). Normally expressed in terms of kb/s (kilobits per second) or Mb/s (megabits per second). For example, the bit rate of a standard CD is (2 channels x 16 bits per sample x 44.1 thousand samples per second) = 1411.2 kilobits/second. Popular MP3 file format bit rates range from 128kb/s to 320kb/s, while the Dolby Digital 5.1 surround soundtrack on a DVD-Video typically ranges between 384 and 448kb/s.

Blumlein array — A stereo-coincident microphone technique devised by English inventor Alan Blumlein in the early 1930s. It employs a pair of microphones with figure-eight polar patterns, mounted at 90 degrees to each other with the two diaphragms vertically aligned.

BNC — A type of bayonet-locking, two-terminal connector used for video and digital audio connections.

Boomy sound - Characterized by pronounced exaggeration of the midbass and, often, dominance of a narrow range of bass frequencies.

Buffer memory — A buffer is essentially a short-term data storage facility used to accommodate variable data read or write periods, temporarily storing data in sequence until it can be processed or transferred by or to some other part of the system.

Bypass test — Directly comparing the output signal from a device with the input signal being fed to it, by putting the device into and then out of the signal path and observing the difference.

Cabinet resonance — Any box-like construction will resonate at one or more frequencies. In the case of a loudspeaker, such resonances are undesirable because they obscure or interfere with the sound from the drive units. Cabinets are usually braced and damped internally to minimize resonance.

Capacitor — A passive, two-terminal electrical component which stores energy in the form of an electrostatic field. The terminals are attached to conductive 'plates' which are separated by a non-conductive dielectric. Capacitance is measured in Farads. If a voltage is applied across the terminals of a capacitor, a static electric field develops across the dielectric, with a positive charge collecting on one plate and a negative charge on the other. When the applied voltage is an alternating signal, a capacitor can be thought of as a form of AC resistance that reduces with increasing signal frequency.

Cardioid — A specific form of polar response in a unidirectional microphone or loudspeaker. It has an inverted heart-shape with very low sensitivity at the back (180 degrees), but only slightly reduced sensitivity, typically between 3 and 6dB, at the sides (90/270 degrees).

Center fill — Correct image placement between the loudspeakers of sound sources which were originally located at or near center-stage.

Center stage — The part of the soundstage that is midway between the loudspeakers.

Chesty sound — A pronounced thickness or heaviness from reproduced male voice, due to excessive energy in the upper bass or lower midrange.

Chip — A slang term for an integrated circuit or IC.

Clinical sound — Pristinely clean but wholly uninvolving.

Clipping — When an audio signal is allowed to overload the system, clipping occurs and severe distortion results. The 'clipping point' is reached when the audio system can no longer accommodate the signal amplitude, whether because an analog signal's voltage nears or exceeds the circuitry's power supply voltage or because a digital sample amplitude exceeds the quantizer's number range. In both cases, the result is that the signal peaks are 'clipped' because the system can't support the peak excursions— a sine wave source signal becomes more like a square wave. In an analog system, clipping produces strong harmonic distortion artifacts at frequencies above the fundamental.

Clocking — The process of controlling the sample rate of one digital device with an external clock signal derived from another device. In a conventional digital system, there can be only one master clock device, with everything else 'clocked' or 'slaved' from that master.

Close-miking —Placing a microphone very close to a sound source, normally with the intention of maximizing the wanted sound and minimizing any unwanted sound from other nearby sound sources or the room acoustics. In classical music circles, the technique is more often known as 'accent miking.'

Coincident — A means of arranging two or more directional microphone capsules such that they receive sound waves from all directions at exactly the same time. The varying sensitivity to sound arriving from different directions, due to the directional polar patterns, means that information about the directions of sound sources is captured in the form of level differences between the capsule outputs. Specific forms of coincident microphones include 'XY' and 'MS' configurations, as well as B-format and Ambisonic arrays. Coincident arrays are entirely mono-compatible because there are no timing differences between channels.

Coloration — A distortion of the natural timbre or frequency response of sound, usually but not always unwanted.

Comb filtering — An undesirable series of deep filter notches created when a signal is combined with a delayed version of itself, causing a hollow coloration to the sound. The delay time (typically less than 10ms) determines the lowest frequency at which the filter notches start.

Common mode rejection — A measure of how well a balanced circuit rejects an interference signal that is common to both sides of the balanced connection.

Conductor — Any material that provides a low-resistance path for electrical current.

Copy protection — A method used by CD and software manufacturers to prevent unauthorized copying (DRM).

CPU — Central Processing Unit, the number-crunching heart of a computer or other data processor.

Crossover — A set of audio filters designed to restrict and control the range of input signal frequencies which are passed to each loudspeaker drive unit. A typical two-way speaker will employ three filters: a high-pass filter that allows only the higher frequencies to feed the tweeter, a low-pass filter that allows only the lower frequencies to feed the woofer, and a second high-pass filter that prevents subsonic signals from damaging the woofer.

Crossover frequency — The frequency at which one driver ceases to produce most of the sound and a second driver takes over. In the case of a two-way speaker, the crossover frequency is usually between 1 and 3kHz.

Cut-off frequency — The frequency above or below which attenuation begins in a filter circuit.

Cycle — One complete vibration (from maximum peak through the negative peak, and back to the maximum again) of a sound source or its electrical equivalent. One cycle per second is expressed as 1 Hertz (Hz).

Damping — The control of a resonant device. In the context of reverberation, damping refers to the rate at which the reverberant energy is absorbed by the various surfaces in the environment. In the context of a loudspeaker it relates to the cabinet design and internal acoustic absorbers. Underdamping causes loose, heavy bass; overdamping yields very tight but lean bass.

Damping factor — The ratio of nominal loudspeaker impedance to the total impedance driving it (amplifier and speaker cable). In practice, damping is the ability of the amplifier to control speaker motion once the signal has stopped. A high damping factor means that the amplifier's impedance can absorb the electricity generated by speaker coil motion, stopping the speaker's vibration.

Dark sound — A warm, mellow, excessively rich quality in reproduced sound.

dB — The deciBel is a method of expressing the ratio between two quantities in a logarithmic fashion, because the logarithmic nature matches the logarithmic character of the human sense of hearing. Decibels are used when comparing one signal level against another (such as the input and output levels of an amplifier or filter). When the two signal amplitudes are the same, the decibel value is 0dB. If one signal has twice the amplitude of the other the decibel value is +6dB, and if half the size it is -6dB.

dB/octave — A means of measuring the slope or steepness of a filter. The gentlest audio filter is typically 6dB/Octave (also called a first-order slope). Higher values indicate sharper filter slopes. 24dB/octave (fourth order) is the steepest normally found in analog audio applications, though far steeper slopes can be achieved with digital filtering techniques through the use of DSP.

DC — Direct Current. The form of electrical current supplied by batteries and the power supplies inside electrical equipment. The current flows in one direction only.

Delicacy of sound — The reproduction of very subtle, faint details of musical sound, such as the sounds produced when a stringed instrument is plucked.

Depth of sound — The illusion of acoustical distance receding behind the loudspeaker plane, giving the impression of listening through the loudspeakers into the original performing space, rather than just listening to the speakers.

Detailed sound — The subtlest, most delicate parts of the original sound, which are easy to lose with the use of low-end equipment and cables.

Diffuse sound — Reproduction which is severely deficient in detail and imaging specificity; confused, muddled.

De-emphasis — A system which restores the spectral balance to correct for pre-emphasis.

Decay — The progressive reduction in amplitude of a sound or electrical signal over time, e.g. the reverb decay of a room.

Decca tree — A form of 'spaced microphone' arrangement in which three microphone capsules (usually, but not always, with omnidirectional polar patterns) are placed in a large triangular array roughly two meters wide, with the central microphone one meter further forward. Sounds approaching from different directions arrive at each capsule at different times and with slightly different levels, and these timing and level differences are used to convey the directional information in the recording. The technique was developed in the early 1950s and was first commercially used in 1954 by Arthur Haddy and Roy Wallace. It was later refined by engineer Kenneth Ernest Wilkinson and his team at Decca Records, to provide a strong stereo image.

Digital audio — A means of representing audio information in the form of binary codes comprised of strings of 1s and 0s, or their electrical or physical equivalents. Digital audio circuitry uses discrete voltages or currents to represent the audio signal at specific moments in time (samples). A properly engineered digital system has infinite resolution, the same as an analog system, but the audio bandwidth is restricted by the sample rate, and the signal-noise ratio (or dynamic range) is restricted by the word-length.

Direct coupling — A means of connecting two electrical circuits so that both AC and DC signals may be passed between them without need of a capacitor.

Dither — An intentionally applied form of noise used to randomize quantization errors used in processing digital audio data. It is often one of the last stages of mastering audio to a CD. Dither must be employed whenever the word length is reduced; otherwise quantizing distortion errors will occur.

Dolby noise-reduction — Dolby is a manufacturer of analog and digital audio equipment in the fields of cinema and surround-sound equipment. Dolby's noise-reduction systems included types B, C, and S for domestic and semi-professional machines, and types A and SR for professional machines. Recordings made using one of these systems must also be replayed through the same system. These systems vary in complexity and effectiveness, but essentially, they all employ the principles of spectral noise-masking in ever-more complex ways, using multiband encode/decode processing to raise low-level signals during recording while reversing the process during playback.

Dolby surround-sound — Dolby's surround-sound systems started with an analogue 4:2:4 phase-matrix system with a very elaborate active-steering decoder called ProLogic, before moving into the digital realm with Dolby Digital, Dolby Digital Plus, Dolby True HD, and others.

DSD — Direct Stream Digital, invented by Sony and Philips for their introduction of the SACD. DSD uses pulse-density modulation encoding. The signal is stored as delta-sigma modulated digital audio, a sequence of single-bit values at a sampling rate of 2.8224 MHz (64 times the CD audio sampling rate of 44.1 kHz, but only at 1/32768 of its 16-bit resolution). Noise shaping occurs by use of the 64-times oversampled signal to reduce noise and distortion, caused by the inaccuracy of quantizing the audio signal to a single bit.

DSP — Digital Signal Processor. A powerful microchip used to process digital audio signals.

Dynamic range — The amplitude range, usually expressed in decibels, between the loudest signal that can be handled by a piece of equipment and the level at which small signals disappear into the noise floor.

Dynamics — A way of describing the relative levels within a piece of music.

Early reflections — The initial sound reflections from walls, floors, and ceilings following a sound created in an acoustically reflective environment.

Encode/decode — A system that modifies a signal prior to recording or transmission, then subsequently restores the signal on playback or reception.

Etched sound — Very crisp and sharply outlined, focused to an almost excessive degree.

Euphonic sound — Pleasing to the ear. In audio, "euphonic" has a connotation of exaggerated richness rather than literal accuracy.

Equalizer — A device which allows the user to adjust the tonality of a sound source by boosting or attenuating a specific range of frequencies. Equalizers are available in the form of shelf equalizers, parametric equalizers, and graphic equalizers—or as a combination of these basic forms.

Equivalent input noise — A means of describing the intrinsic electronic noise at the output of an amplifier in terms of an equivalent input noise, taking into account the amplifier's gain.

Fat sound — The sonic effect of a moderate exaggeration of the mid- and upper-bass ranges. Excessively "warm."

FET — Field Effect Transistor. A solid-state semiconductor device in which the current flowing between the source and drain terminals is controlled by the voltage on the gate terminal. The FET is a very high-impedance device with a warm and tube-like sonic characteristic when used in an audio circuit.

Fidelity — The accuracy or precision of a reproduced acoustic sound wave when compared to the electrical input signal.

Filter frequency — The 'turnover' or 'corner' frequency of a high- or low-pass filter. Technically, the frequency at which the signal amplitude has been attenuated by 3dB.

Flash drive — A portable, large-capacity, solid-state memory stick configured to work like a conventional hard drive. Some computers and music servers are now available with solid state flash drives, SSDs, instead of normal internal hard drives.

Floppy disk — An obsolete computer disk format using a flexible magnetic medium encased in a protective plastic sleeve.

Flutter — A high-speed variation in replay speed causing rapid 'fluttering' pitch variations.

Focused sound — The quality of being clearly defined, with sharply outlined phantom images. Focus has also been described as the enhanced ability to hear the brief moments of silence between the musical impulses in reproduced sound.

Forward sound — A quality of reproduction which seems to place sound sources closer than they were recorded. Usually the result of a humped midrange, plus a narrow horizontal dispersion pattern from the loudspeaker.

Frequency range — A range of frequencies stated without level limits: e.g., "the upper bass covers the frequency range 80-160Hz."

Frequency response — A range of frequencies stated with level limits. The uniformity with which a system or individual component sounds as if it reproduces the range of audible frequencies. Equal input levels at all frequencies should be reproduced by a system with subjectively equal output.

Fundamental — The lowest frequency component in a harmonically complex sound.

Gain — The amount by which a circuit amplifies a signal, normally noted in decibels.

Galvanic isolation — Electrical isolation between two circuits. A transformer provides galvanic isolation because there is no direct electrical connection between the primary and secondary windings; the audio signal is passed via magnetic coupling. An opto-coupler also provides galvanic isolation, as the signal is passed via light modulation.

Glare — An unpleasant quality of hardness or brightness, due to excessive low- or mid-treble energy.

Glassy sound — Very bright.

Golden sound — A euphonic coloration characterized by roundness, richness, sweetness, and liquidity.

Grainy sound — A moderate texturing of reproduced sound. The sonic equivalent of grain in a photograph. Coarser than dry but finer than gritty.

Gritty sound — A harsh, coarse-grained texturing of reproduced sound. The continuum of energy seems to be composed of discrete, sharp-edged particles.

Graphic equalizer — An equalizer with multiple narrow segments of the audio spectrum are controlled by individual cut/boost faders. The name came about because the fader positions provide a graphic representation of the EQ curve.

Ground — An alternative term for the electrical Earth or o Volts reference. In electrical wiring, the ground cable is often physically connected to the planet's surface via a long conductive metal spike. In an audio device, ground is often the chassis or the center tap of the power transformer.

Ground loop/ground loop hum — A condition created when two or more devices are interconnected in such a way that a loop of varying potential is created in the ground circuit. This can result in audible hums or buzzes in analog equipment or unreliability and audio glitches in digital equipment. Typically, a ground loop is created when two devices are connected together using one or more shielded audio cables, and both units are also plugged into the mains supply with safety ground connections via the mains' plug earth pins. The loop exists between one mains plug, to the first device, through the audio cable shield to the second device, back to the mains supply via the second mains plug, and around to the first device via the building's power wiring.

GUI — Graphical User Interface (pronounced 'gooey'). In computer software, a GUI is a visual operating environment controlled by a mouse-driven pointer or something similar.

Hard disk drive — The conventional means of computer data storage: one or more metal disks (hard disks) hermetically sealed in an enclosure with integral drive electronics and interfacing. The disks are coated in a magnetic material and spun at high speed (typically 7200rpm for audio applications). A series of movable arms carrying miniature magnetic heads are arranged to move closely over the surface of the discs, to record (write) and replay (read) data.

Harmonic — High-frequency components of a complex waveform, where the harmonic frequency is an integer multiple of the fundamental.

Harmonic distortion — The addition of harmonics (multiple higher frequencies of the fundamental) that were not present in the original signal, caused by non-linearities in an electronic circuit or audio transducer.

Headroom — The available 'safety margin' in audio equipment required to accommodate unexpectedly loud audio transient signals. It is defined as the region between the nominal operating level (0VU) and the clipping point.

Height — Vertical directional cues which make some instruments sound as if they are above or below the other performers.

Hertz (Hz) — The standard measurement of frequency. 10Hz means ten complete cycles of a repeating waveform per second.

High-pass filter (HPF) — A filter which passes frequencies above its cut-off frequency but attenuates lower frequencies.

High-range (highs) — The upper portion of the audible frequency spectrum, typically denoting frequencies above about 1kHz.

High resolution — A digital format with long word-lengths and high sample rates, e.g. 24/96 or 24/192. Word-length defines the system's signal-to-noise ratio and dynamic capabilities, while sample rate defines the maximum audio bandwidth possible.

Hiss —**Noise** caused by random electrical fluctuations (or by annoying a cat).

Hub — Normally used in the context of the USB–computer data interface. A hub is a device used to expand a single USB port into several, enabling the connection of multiple devices. Particularly useful where multiple software program authorization dongles must be connected to the computer.

Hum — Audio signal contamination caused by the addition of low frequencies, usually related to the mains power frequency.

Hysteresis — When the system's output lags behind the input. Most commonly found in audio in the behavior of ferro-magnetic materials, such as in transformers and analog tape heads, or in electronic circuits such as 'switch de-bouncing.'

IC — An abbreviation of Integrated Circuit, a collection of miniaturized transistors and other components on a single silicon wafer, designed to perform a specific function.

Imaging — The measure of a system's ability to float stable and specific phantom images, reproducing the original sizes and locations of the instruments across the soundstage.

Impact — A quality of concussive force, as from a deep, strong bass attack, which produces a brief sensation of visceral pressure.

Impulse — An abrupt, extremely brief burst of signal energy; a transient.

Impedance — The 'resistance' or opposition of a medium to a change of state, often encountered in the context of electrical connections (and the way signals of different frequencies are treated) or acoustic treatment (denoting the resistance it presents to air flow). Although measured in Ohms, the impedance of a 'reactive' device such as a loudspeaker drive unit will usually vary with signal frequency and will be higher than the resistance when measured with a static DC voltage. Signal sources have an output impedance and destinations have an input impedance. In analog audio systems, the usual arrangement is to source from a very low impedance and feed a destination of a much higher impedance (typically 10 times as high).

Impulse response — An impulse response is the time-domain equivalent of the much more familiar frequency (and phase) responses in the frequency domain. A very brief click (technically, a Dirac delta function), which theoretically contains all frequencies at equal amplitude, is passed through the device being tested. The resulting output is the 'impulse response' of that device and uniquely describes its signal processing behavior. Impulse responses are very convenient for digital signal processing applications, as the source impulse is very similar to a single digital sample value.

Inductor — A magnetic reactive component that presents an increasing impedance with frequency. These are typically coils of wire used in speakers as low-pass filters, limiting high frequency signals.

Infrasonic — Below the range of audible frequencies. Although inaudible, the infrasonic range from 15-20Hz can be felt if strongly reproduced.

Inner detail — The sonic subtleties within a complex program signal, reproducible only by a system having high resolution.

Input impedance — The input impedance of an electrical network is the 'load' into which a power source delivers energy. In modern audio systems the input impedance is normally about ten times higher than the source impedance—a typical audio preamplifier or source component has an output impedance of 100 ohm, while input impedance is typically 10k ohm to 30k ohm.

Insulator — Any material that does not conduct electricity.

Intermittent — Something that happens occasionally and unpredictably, typically a fault condition in audio troubleshooting.

Intermodulation distortion — A form of non-linear distortion that introduces frequencies absent from and musically unrelated to the original signal. They are invariably based on the sum and difference products of the original frequencies.

I/O — The input/output connections of a system.

Isolator — A device intended to prevent the transmission of physical vibrations over a specific frequency range, such as a rubber or foam block. The term can also be applied to audio isolation transformers, used to provide galvanic isolation between the source and destination, thus avoiding ground loops.

Latency — The time delay experienced between a sound or control signal being generated and it being auditioned or taking effect, measured in seconds.

LED — Light Emitting Diode. A form of solid-state lamp.

LCD — Liquid Crystal Display.

Lean sound — Very slightly bass-shy. The effect of a slight bass rolloff below around 500Hz.

Lifeless sound — Sound that is dull, unfocused, unconvincing, and uninvolving.

LSB — Least Significant Byte (or bit). If a piece of data has to be conveyed as two bytes, one byte represents high-value numbers and the other low-value numbers, in much the same way as tens and ones function in the decimal system. The high-value, or most significant part of the message, is called the Most Significant Byte or MSB.

Linear — A device where the output is a direct multiple of the input, with no unwanted distortions.

Line-level — A nominal signal level which is around -10dBV for consumer audio and +4dBu for professional equipment.

Listening fatigue — A psychoacoustic phenomenon caused by prolonged listening to sound whose nature leans towards harsh, bright, or aggressive. The physical and psychological discomfort can induce headaches and nervous tension.

Low-pass filter (LPF) — A filter which passes frequencies below its cut-off frequency but attenuates higher frequencies.

Loudspeaker — A device used to convert an electrical audio signal into an acoustic sound wave. An accurate loudspeaker intended for critical sound auditioning purposes.

Loudness — The perceived volume of an audio signal.

Loudness wars — The practice of trying to make each new commercial music release sound subjectively louder than any previous release, based on the misguided notion that louder music is more exciting and results in more sales. A relationship between the average loudness of 45rpm singles and sales was noticed in America from jukebox plays, and that led to the first loudness war. However, the advent of the CD really ramped up the situation, with music being ever-more dynamically compressed to squeeze the average level higher and higher towards the 0dBFS peak level. This destructive trend is, thankfully, now being slowly reversed with the ubiquity of loudness normalization adopted by most online audio streaming services and broadcasters.

Low-level detail — The subtlest elements of musical sound, which include the delicate details of instrumental sounds and the final tail of reverberation decay.

Lumpy sound — Reproduced sound characterized by a number of audible response discontinuities through the range below about 1kHz. Certain frequency bands seem to predominate, while others sound weak.

Lush sound — Rich-sounding and sumptuous to the point of excess.

Mastering — Traditionally, the sequencing of individual recordings to form a cohesive album of material, and to apply corrective equalization and dynamics processing that ensures a consistent sound character and optimizes playback on the widest possible range of sound systems. Appropriate signal processing may also be applied to make the mastered material suitable for its intended medium (such as controlling transient peaks and dynamics and monoing the bass for vinyl records).

Maximum SPL — The loudest sound pressure level that a device can generate or tolerate.

Midbass — The range of frequencies from 40-80Hz.

Mineral wool — Wool made from natural or synthetic minerals in the form of threads or fibers, tangled together to form a moderately dense 'blanket' which permits but impedes air flow. It is useful in the creation of sound absorbers, so is often employed as a cheaper and more efficient alternative to polyurethane form.

Mirror points — The positions on the walls or ceiling where, if the surface were covered with an optical mirror, one or both loudspeakers could be seen in the reflection. The mirror point is essentially any position on a boundary where sound waves from a sound source—usually a monitor loudspeaker—will be reflected directly to the listening position. This is traditionally the ideal location to place an acoustic absorber to prevent audible reflections.

Modal distribution — The characteristic distribution of resonant low frequency sound waves within a confined space such as a room.

Mono — A single channel of audio.

Monophonic — One note at a time.

Muddy sound — Ill-defined, congested.

Musicality — A personal judgment as to the degree to which reproduced sound resembles live music. Real musical sound is both accurate and euphonic, consonant and dissonant.

Nasal sound — Reproduced sound having the quality of a person speaking with his/her nose blocked. In a loudspeaker, it is often due to a measured peak in the upper midrange followed by a complementary dip.

Near-coincident — A means of arranging two or more directional microphone capsules so they receive sound waves from different directions at slightly different times, due to their physical spacing. Information about the directions of sound sources is captured in the form of both level differences between the capsule outputs, generated by aiming directional polar patterns in different directions, and the timing differences caused by their physical spacing.

Near field — The acoustic zone close to a sound source or microphone. Often used to describes a loudspeaker system designed to be used close to the listener, although some people prefer the term 'close field.' The advantage is that the listener hears more of the direct sound from the speakers and less of the reflected sound from the room.

Noise-shaping — A system using spectrally-shaped dither to improve the perceived signal-to-noise performance of a digital audio system. Often used in DSD and modern DACs.

Nyquist Theorem — This rule states that a digital sampling system must have a sample rate at least twice as high as that of the highest audio frequency being sampled, in order to avoid aliasing and thus reproduce the desired audio perfectly. Because anti-aliasing filters aren't perfect, the sampling frequency usually has to be slightly more than twice that of the maximum input frequency— which is why the standard audio rate of 44.1kHz was chosen for a nominally 20kHz audio bandwidth.

Octave — When a frequency or pitch is transposed up by one octave, its frequency is doubled.

Off-axis/on-axis — Directional microphones are inherently more sensitive to sound from one direction, and the direction of greatest sensitivity is referred to as the principal axis. Sound sources placed on this axis are said to be 'on-axis,' while sound sources elsewhere are said to be 'off-axis.'

Ohm — A standard unit of electrical resistance.

Omnidirectional — A microphone or loudspeaker polar pattern with equal sensitivity in all directions.

Open-sounding — Exhibiting qualities of delicacy, air, and fine detail. Giving an impression of having no upper-frequency limit.

Out-of-phase — In a two-channel system, one channel is out-of-phase if it is in opposite polarity to the second. Most often, this is because one speaker was hooked up with the red (positive) lead to the red (positive) terminal, and the other with the red lead to the black (negative terminal). Along with causing a "phasey" sound, this error will reduce low frequencies.

Open circuit — A break in an electrical circuit that prevents current from flowing.

Output impedance — The effective internal impedance (resistance which may change with signal frequency) of an electronic device. In modern audio equipment, the output impedance is normally very low.

Overload — To exceed the maximum acceptable signal amplitude of an electronic or electrical circuit. Overloading a device results in a noticeable increase in distortion.

Overtone — A component of a complex sound which has a higher frequency than the fundamental frequency, but which is not necessarily related to the fundamental by a simple integer multiple.

Pace and rhythm — The apparent tempo of a musical performance, which can be different from its actual beats-per-minute tempo. Pace is affected by phrasing in performance and speed in reproduction.

Palpable sound — Describes reproduction that is so realistic you feel you could reach out and touch the instruments or singers.

Parallel —A means of connecting two or more circuits together so that their inputs are connected together and their outputs are connected together.

Parameter — A variable value that affects some aspect of a device's performance.

Parametric EQ — An equalizer with separate controls for frequency, bandwidth, and cut/boost.

Passive circuit — A circuit with no active elements.

Passive loudspeaker — A loudspeaker which requires an external power amplifier, the signal from which is passed to a passive cross-over filter.

PCM — Pulse Code Modulation, the technique used by most digital audio systems to encode audio as binary data.

Peak level — The maximum instantaneous level of a signal.

Phantom image — The re-creation by a stereo system of an apparent sound source at a location other than that of either loudspeaker.

Phase — The relative position of a point within a cyclical signal, expressed in degrees, where 360 degrees corresponds to one full cycle.

Phono plug (RCA-phono) — An audio connector developed by RCA and used extensively on Hi-Fi and semi-pro, unbalanced audio equipment. Also used for the electrical form of S/PDIF digital signals, and occasionally for video signals.

Pinched sounding — A laterally compressed soundstage lacking in spaciousness.

Pinpoint imaging — Stereo imaging that is precise, stable, and focused.

Polar pattern — The directional characteristic of a microphone (omni, cardioid, figure-eight, etc.).

Polarity — This refers to a signal's voltage above or below the median line. Inverting the polarity of a signal swaps the positive voltage to negative voltage and vice versa. This condition is often referred to as 'out-of-phase.'

Potentiometer (Pot) — A form of electrical potential divider in which the ratio of the upper and lower resistances can be changed, either with a rotary control or slider, for the purpose of lowering or raising volume levels.

Power amplifier — A device which accepts a standard line-level input signal and amplifies it to a condition in which it can drive a loudspeaker drive unit. The strength of amplification is denoted in terms of watts of power.

Power supply — A unit designed to convert mains electricity to the DC voltages necessary to power an electronic circuit or device.

Powered loudspeaker or monitor — A powered speaker is a conventional passive loudspeaker that includes a single (or multiple) power amplifier built into or integrated with the cabinet in some way. The amplifier drives a passive crossover, the outputs of which connect to the appropriate drive units.

Pre-amp — Short for pre-amplification: an active gain stage used to select the input source and raise the signal level of a source to a nominal line level.

Pre-emphasis — A system for applying high-frequency boost to a sound before processing. When the corresponding de-emphasis is applied, any noise contribution from the processing is reduced.

Presence — Sounding realistic, alive.

Print-through — An undesirable process that causes some magnetic information from a recorded analog tape to become imprinted onto an adjacent layer. This can produce low level pre- or post-echoes.

Q — The 'quality-factor' of a filter which defines its bandwidth and indicates a filter's resonant properties. The higher the Q, the more resonant the filter is and the narrower the range of frequencies that are allowed to pass.

Quantization — Part of the process of digitizing an analog signal. Quantization is the process of describing or measuring the amplitude of the analog signal captured in each sample, and it is defined by the word length used to describe the audio signal, e.g. 16 bits.

RAM — Random Access Memory, a type of memory used by computers for the temporary storage of programs and data. Because all data stored in RAM is deleted when the power is turned off, work needs to be saved to a hard drive or external disk to protect it.

Red book CD — A standard audio CD. The name comes from the fact that the original specification documents for the audio CD created by Sony and Philips had a red cover. Recordable CD-Rs are described as 'orange book' for similar reasons.

Reflection — The way in which sound waves bounce off surfaces.

Resistance — Opposition to the flow of electrical current, measured in ohms.

Resonance — The characteristic of a filter that allows it to selectively pass a narrow range of frequencies.

Reverb — Short for reverberation. The dense collection of echoes which bounce off acoustically reflective surfaces in response to direct sound arriving from a signal source. Reverberation occurs a short while after the source signal because of the finite time it takes the sound to reach a reflective surface and return—the overall delay is representative of the size of the acoustic environment. A reverberation signal has two main components: a group of distinct 'early reflections' followed by a noise-like tail of dense reflections.

Revealing sound — Pertaining to a loudspeaker or a system as a whole: Outstandingly detailed and focused.

Reverberation time — The time taken for sound waves reflecting within a space to lose energy and become inaudible. A standard measurement is

'RT60,' which is the time taken for the sound reflections to decay by 60dB.

RF —Radio Frequency.

RF interference — Unwanted interference in an audio system from external radio frequency signals.

Ribbon microphone — A dynamic microphone where the sound-capturing element is a thin metal ribbon diaphragm suspended within a magnetic field. When sound causes the ribbon to vibrate, a small electrical current is generated within the ribbon.

RMS — Root Mean Square, a statistical measure of the magnitude of a varying quantity. Its name comes from its definition: the square root of the mean of the squares of the values of the signal.

Roll-off — The rate at which a filter or equalizer attenuates a signal once it has passed the turnover frequency.

Rolloff — A frequency response which falls gradually above or below a certain frequency limit. By comparison, the term cutoff (often abbreviated to "cut," as in "bass cut") implies an abrupt loss of level above or below the frequency limit.

Rotary encoder — A hardware controller featuring a knob or dial which can be rotated in either direction without end-stops. A digital encoder of some kind attached to the shaft translates the movement into a digital code, which can indicate both the direction and speed of rotation to the controlling software of a device and thus control the volume of a stereo product.

Rumble — An extraneous low-frequency noise, often of indeterminate pitch, caused by the physical vibration of a turntable or of the room in which a recording was made.

SACD — Super Audio CD, a read-only optical disc format for audio storage, based on the 1-bit DSD format. It was developed jointly in 1999 by Sony and Philips Electronics, who intended it to be the successor to the Compact Disc (CD) format. SACDs, though sonically superior to CDs, did not achieve the same level of growth that CDs enjoyed in the 1980s, and they were not accepted by the mainstream market. By 2007, SACD format had failed to make a significant impact in the marketplace: consumers were increasingly downloading low-resolution music files over the internet rather than buying music on physical disc formats. A small and niche market for SACD has remained, serving the audiophile community.

Sample rate — The number of times an A/D converter samples the incoming waveform each second.

Seamless sound — Having no perceptible discontinuities throughout the audio range.

Short-circuit — An undesirably low resistance path allowing electrical current to flow, typically with bad results, e.g. shorting the output terminals of a power amplifier. The term is usually used to describe a current path that exists through a fault condition.

Sibilance — A high-frequency whistling or lisping sound that affects vocal recordings, due either to poor mic technique or excessive HF equalization.

Signal — An electrical representation of an audio event.

Signal chain — The route taken by a signal from the input of a system to the output.

Signal-to-noise ratio — The ratio of nominal or maximum signal level to the residual noise floor, expressed in decibels.

Silky sound — Describes treble performance that is velvety-smooth, delicate, and open.

Sine wave — The waveform of a pure sinusoidal tone with no harmonics.

Sizzly sound — Sound emphasizing the frequency range above about 8kHz, which adds sibilance to all sounds, particularly those of cymbals and vocal sibilants.

Slam — Impact.

Smeared sound — Severe lack of detail and focus.

Solid-state drive (SSD) — A large capacity, solid-state memory block configured to work like a conventional hard disk drive.

Sound card — A dedicated interface to transfer audio signals in and out of a computer. A sound card can be installed internally or connected externally via USB or FireWire, and they are available in a wide range of formats, accommodating multiple analog or digital audio signals (or both) in and out.

Soundstaging — The accuracy with which a reproduction system conveys audible information about the size, shape, and acoustical characteristics of the original recording space and the placement of the performers within it.

S/PDIF — Sony/Philips Digital Interface, a stereo or dual-channel self-clocking digital interfacing standard employed by Sony and Philips in consumer digital Hi-Fi products. The S/PDIF signal is essentially identical in data format to the professional AES3 interface, and it is available as either an unbalanced electrical interface (using phono connectors and a 75ohm coaxial cable) or as an optical interface called TOSlink.

Speed — The apparent rapidity with which a reproduction system responds to steep wavefronts and overall musical pace.

SPL — Sound Pressure Level, a measure of the intensity of an acoustic sound wave. Normally specified in terms of pascals for an absolute value, or relative to the typical sensitivity of human hearing. One pascal is 94dB SPL, or to relate it to atmospheric pressures, 0.00001 Bar or 0.000145psi.

Square wave — A symmetrical rectangular waveform. Square waves contain a series of odd harmonics.

Standing waves — Resonant low-frequency sound waves bouncing between opposite surfaces, such that each reflected wave aligns perfectly with previous waves, to create static areas of maximum and minimum sound pressure within the room.

State-of-the-art — Describes equipment whose performance is as good as the technology allows. The best sound equipment money can buy.

Stereo — By convention, two channels of related audio which can create the impression of separate sound source positions when auditioned on a pair of loudspeakers or headphones.

Strident — Unpleasantly shrill, piercing.

Subsonic — Slower than the speed of sound through air. Often used incorrectly to mean infrasonic.

Subwoofer — A specific type of efficient loudspeaker system intended to reproduce only the lowest frequencies (typically below 120Hz).

Surge — A sudden increase in mains voltage.

Subjectivist — A person who has found that measurements don't tell the whole story about reproduced sound.

Surround sound — The use of multiple loudspeakers, placed around the listening position, with the aim of reproducing a sense of envelopment within a soundstage. Numerous surround formats exist, but the most common currently is the 5.1 configuration in which three loudspeakers are placed in front of the listener (at ±30 degrees and straight ahead) and two behind (at ±120 degrees or thereabouts), supplemented with a separate subwoofer.

Sweet spot — That listening seat from which the best soundstage presentation is heard. Usually a center seat equidistant from the loudspeakers.

Switching power supply (SMPS) — A type of power supply that uses mains power to directly drive a high-frequency oscillator, so that a smaller, lighter transformer may be used. These power supplies are commonly used because they can be made to accept a wide range of mains supply voltages and are thus universal.

Tempo — The rate of the 'beat' of a piece of music, measured in beats per minute.

Test tone — A steady, fixed-level tone recorded onto a multitrack recording, or passed over a signal connection, to test the signal path and act as a reference when matching levels.

Textured sound — A perceptible pattern or structure in reproduced sound, even if random in nature. Texturing gives the impression that the energy continuum of the sound is composed of discrete particles, like the grain of a photograph.

Thick sound — Describes sodden or heavy bass.

Thin sound — Very deficient in bass. The result of severe attenuation of the range below 500Hz.

THD — Total Harmonic Distortion, a measure of the linearity of a device. The THD+N measurement, which also includes the noise contribution, is one indication of the quality of an audio product.

Tizzy sound — An exaggerated high-frequency coloration of the sound of cymbals and vocal sibilants, caused by a rising frequency response above 10kHz.

Transformer — An electrical device in which two or more separate and electrically isolated coils of wire are wound around a common ferromagnetic core. Alternating current passing through one coil creates a varying magnetic field which induces a corresponding current in the other coil(s). In audio applications, transformers are often used to convey a signal without a direct electrical connection, thus providing 'galvanic isolation' between the source and destination. Winding a transformer with different numbers of turns for each coil allows the output voltage to be increased or decreased in direct proportion— a feature widely employed in mains power-supply transformers to reduce the mains voltage to something more appropriate for the circuitry, for example, or in microphone preamp step-up transformers.

Transients — An element of a sound where the spectral content changes abruptly. Most natural sounds start with a transient element before settling into something more steady-state, and that transient element often provides most of the recognizable character of the sound source.

Transparency — A subjective term used to describe audio quality where the high-frequency detail is clear and individual sounds are easy to identify and separate. A quality of sound reproduction that gives the impression of listening through the system to the original sounds, rather than to a pair of loudspeakers.

Tubby sound — Having an exaggerated deep-bass range.

Tweeter — The colloquial term to describe a loudspeaker drive unit optimized for the reproduction of high frequencies.

Unbalanced signal — A two-wire electrical signal connection, typically using RCA connectors, where the signal conductor is surrounded by a shield which provides a 0V reference and also guards against electrical interference.

Uninvolving sound — "Meh" sound. Reproduction which evokes boredom and indifference.

Upper bass — The range of frequencies from 80-160Hz.

Unity gain — A condition where the output signal is the same amplitude as the input signal; the overall system gain is then x1 or unity.

USB — Universal Serial Bus, a computer interface standard introduced in 1996 to replace the previously standard serial and parallel ports. The USB 1.1 interface operated at up to 12Mb/s, but this was superseded in 2000 by USB 2.0 which operates at up to 480Mb/s. Most USB interfaces can also provide a 5V power supply to connected devices. USB 3.0 was launched in 2008 and is claimed to operate at rates up to 5Gb/s.

Valve — Also known as a vacuum tube. A thermionic device in which the current flowing between its anode and cathode terminals is controlled by the voltage applied to one or more control grid(s). Valves can be used as the active elements in amplifiers. The modern solid-state equivalent is the Field Effect Transistor or FET.

Veiled sound — A deficiency of detail and focus, due to moderate amounts of distortion, treble-range restriction, or attack rounding.

VU meter — An audio meter designed to interpret signal levels in roughly the same way as the human ear, which responds more closely to the average levels of sounds than to the peak levels.

Warm sound — The same as dark sound, but less tilted. A certain amount of warmth is a normal part of musical sound.

Watt (W) — A standard unit of electrical power.

Warmth — A subjective term used to describe sound where the bass and low mid frequencies have depth and where the high frequencies are smooth-sounding, rather than being aggressive or fatiguing. Warm-sounding tube equipment may also exhibit some aspects of compression.

Waveform — A graphic representation of how a sound wave or electrical wave varies with time.

Withdrawn sound — Very laid-back.

Woolly sound — Describes loose, ill-defined bass.

Word clock — The precise timing of digital audio samples is critical to the correct operation of interconnected digital audio equipment. The 'metronome' that governs sample timing is called the word clock (sometimes conjoined to 'wordclock' or abbreviated to 'wclk'). However, word clock does more than merely beat time; it also identifies the start and end of each digital word or sample and which samples belong to the left or right channels. Digital interfaces such as the AES3 and S/PDIF embody clock signals within the data stream, but it is often necessary to convey a discrete word clock between equipment as a square wave signal running at the sampling rate. Dedicated word clock inputs and outputs on digital equipment generally use BNC connectors.

XLR — A very robust and latching connector (also colloquially known as an XLR cable), commonly used to carry balanced audio signals between stereo equipment.

Zero crossing point — The point at which a signal waveform crosses from being positive to negative or vice versa.

Notes

Copyright © 2020 Paul McGowan.

Made in the USA
Monee, IL
14 January 2021

57652785R00118